# MIRACLE IN THE MOUNTAINS

*Experiencing the Transforming Power of Faith in the Heart of Appalachia*

by Lonnie and Belinda Riley
with Joyce Sweeney Martin

Library of Congress Control Number: 2010923657

This book is dedicated to the volunteers who have served our Lord
in the heart of Appalachia and to the individuals
who have supported us with their generous financial gifts

# TABLE OF CONTENTS

# Foreword

*I* first met Lonnie Riley in a hallway at Ridgecrest Conference Center near Asheville, North Carolina, in the summer of 1992. He thanked me for my role in writing *Experiencing God: Knowing and Doing the Will of God*. Then he proceeded to tell me of significant transformations that had been taking place in his life, his family, his ministry, his church, and in his community over the past nine months. I asked him to share some of his stories with the class I was teaching at the conference center that summer. I realized that Lonnie was beginning to experience God's activity in ways similar to the ways Henry Blackaby had experienced God.

That day, Lonnie told me about two people who had quit their jobs and walked by faith in the ministries to which God was calling them. He shared how God had provided for them and their ministries financially. Within two months, I was facing an invitation from God that would require me to quit my job and walk by faith to write *Fresh Encounter: God's Pattern for Revival and Spiritual Awakening* with Henry Blackaby. God used Lonnie's stories to increase my faith to believe God in my crisis of belief. I resigned my job at the Baptist Sunday School Board that September with no knowledge of how God would provide for my family… but with great clarity and confidence that He had called and guided me. And God provided!

I began telling Lonnie's stories (along with many others) as I taught about experiencing God and revival around the country. Frequently, people would ask, "Where are these stories written down?" and I would have to respond, "Nowhere." I did record some of Lonnie's story in *Fresh Encounter*. I've found that stories of God's miraculous activity increase the faith of others to believe God when He calls them to walk by faith. I learned that one experientially!

One day, I had the privilege of teaching an "Experiencing God Conference" in Ohio, and I got to see first hand what God was doing. I met a young couple who had come to faith in Christ during this period of transformation for the Rileys. As I talked with them, I was amazed at their faith to believe that their God could do ANYTHING. Isn't that the way God wants us to live?

Later, Lonnie called me about an invitation he had received to teach *Experiencing God* in the Philippines. He said, "I think you are the one who is supposed to go." I wasn't sure, but we prayed. I mentioned that "story" at a meeting in Plattsburgh, New York, and a Filipino talked with me about the needs and opportunities in the Philippines. Before long, *Experiencing God* was being printed in the Philippines. After that, a Filipino leader in New York City and I traveled there and introduced the message to 1,157 pastors and small-group leaders in five major cities. God guided and provided through the whole process in wonderful ways.

Throughout those early years, I talked with Lonnie to get an update on what God was doing. I was always so encouraged. One rarity about Lonnie's testimonies has been the way in which he correctly gives God all the credit. Too often, those who experience God's miraculous activity begin to claim credit and touch His glory; but I've not seen nor heard that from Lonnie.

Then years passed and I lost contact with Lonnie. I returned to work at LifeWay Christian Resources (the former Sunday School Board I had left twelve years before) and Lonnie's name resurfaced. I was serving as an editor with John Franklin as he developed the message for *By Faith: Living in the Certainty of God's Reality*. One day, John called me and explained how he thought he should include Lonnie Riley as a co-author. He gave me a CD with some of Lonnie's stories about the miracle in the mountains of eastern Kentucky in the heart of

Appalachia. Wow! Again, I was hearing testimonies that pointed glory to God. Those are some of the stories you are about to read.

When we began to revise the *Experiencing God* course and capture testimonies, Lonnie was first on my list of prospects to interview. Our video crew spent a day in Lynch, Kentucky, with Lonnie and Belinda. Reading or hearing a story about what God can do is wonderful and encouraging, but seeing the evidence first hand is more so. God is using the stories of His work in Lynch to stir many others to respond to His invitations that require a walk of faith.

That's why I'm thrilled that Joyce Martin has worked with Lonnie and Belinda to testify through this book to what God is doing to reveal His glory. You will be inspired and encouraged as you read the stories. As you read, God's Spirit may speak to you about an invitation He has for *you* to serve Him. Or God may increase your faith to believe Him for the impossibilities in your circumstances. The practical principles Lonnie and Belinda have learned and shared may help guide you in your own walk of faith. The one deficiency of this book is that even with the fact that at least fifty-seven stories are included, you'll not read half of what God has done in Appalachia. You'll be hungry for more.

That's where you come in. I pray that the Lord will use these testimonies of His mighty power to work in and through your life of faith to reveal Himself to the watching world around you. When He works, tell His story; give Him glory!

Claude V. King
Co-author of *Experiencing God: Knowing and Doing the Will of God*
Murfreesboro, Tennessee

# Preface

*During* the last eighteen years, we have experienced the transforming power of faith as God has changed us from "make-it-happen," driven people into "living-by-faith" people. Fueled by crises, failure, and a deep-seated desire to experience God, we were brought to a place of complete surrender to and dependence on Him.

But it was when He called us to leave a comfortable lifestyle and move back home to hard-scrabble Lynch, Kentucky, in the heart of the Appalachian Mountains that we really began to experience what the faith-life is all about. Over and over during the last ten years we have seen God do things only He can do in response to the faith of His people. We have experienced miracle after miracle in the mountains.

During these years, more than thirty thousand volunteers have come to Lynch to minister alongside us and to experience what only God can do. Often, volunteers and friends have asked us to compile a book of stories of the mighty movement of God in the heart of Appalachia. This book, which contains more than fifty stories, is the result of those requests. For clarity, the book is written in Lonnie's voice.

This book is organized around sayings that we have used as we have had the privilege of speaking in the United States, Eastern Europe, and Africa about God-at-work in Appalachia and about how to live the faith-life. These sayings not only give structure to the stories but also illustrate biblical faith-living principles that are the heart of what it means for a believer in Jesus the Christ to experience God's transforming power and to live the faith-life. For readers who wish to study what the Bible teaches about these faith-living principles, the book *By Faith: Living in the Certainty of God's Reality* will be an excellent resource. (For more information, see the Resources page at the end of this book.)

We are convinced that Scripture admonishes God's people to live by faith and not by sight. This is God's "normal" for His followers. It is our prayer that as you read the stories of God's mighty acts in Appalachia and as you ponder the faith principles in this book, the Holy Spirit will lead you to live the "normal" faith-life as well. Scripture teaches that to live by faith is the one response God requires of every believer if He is to show Himself strong in a believer's daily life. We pray that you will allow faith to be the fuel that keeps your relationship with God fresh and releases His power to work in your life. If you do, then you, too, will experience things that you will only be able to explain by saying that "God did it." You, too, will experience the transforming power of faith.

We want to thank those who have been instrumental in our personal faith formation. First and foremost, we give all praise and thanks to our Lord Jesus Christ for invading our lives, forgiving us, teaching us, and walking with us through the storms and the still-water times. We thank God for our children, Lisa, Brian, and Amy, and for how they have taught us much about faith.

We wish to thank Dr. Henry Blackaby, whom God used to introduce us to the faith-life and who has been our mentor and role model for many years. Thank you, Claude King, for writing the foreword to this book. Thanks also goes to Dr. Larry Martin, who has become our mentor and dear friend; to Joyce Sweeney Martin, who has put our thoughts into the words of this book; and to the great host of volunteers from around the world who have served alongside us in the mountains and who flesh out the principles of the faith-life each day.

All that has happened in Lynch over the past ten years can only be explained by saying, "It had nothing to do with any human being, but everything to do with God." All praise belongs to Him.

"The poor and needy are thirsty, but there is no water.
But I, the God of heaven, have heard them.
I will make a river to flow from the mountains
so that all men will know that God has done this thing."
Isaiah 41:17, 20 (Lonnie's paraphrase)

Lonnie and Belinda Riley
Lynch, Kentucky
January 2010

# ONE

~~~~~~~~~~~

# "MAKE IT HAPPEN"

*"Preacher,"* the eight-year-old lad asked, "I just want to know one thing. Are the stories you are telling really true?"

I had finished a message in which I had talked about all the wonderful ways God accomplishes His plan in the world and had shared several stories of God's miraculous intervention in the community where my wife, Belinda, and I live. Then I had asked for questions from the group that had gathered in a church in Bardstown, Kentucky. Quickly, that little hand had shot up—the only hand to be raised, in fact. I turned to the young man and said, "Yes, young man. What is your question?" Without hesitation, he responded. Everybody laughed. I replied, "Yes, those stories are really true, and you can come to Lynch, Kentucky, and see those stories for real."

I then said this to the audience: "This young man asked the question that probably 90 percent of the adults here wanted to ask but were afraid to ask. You know, in New Testament times a person who lived by faith would have found the things I have shared to be normal, but in our society if a person lives by faith, he or she becomes 'abnormal,' and people question whether the things they share are really true. When I share stories of faith, I want the stories to be an encouragement to believers to be normal. From God's perspective, the normal life is the life of faith."

⤙⤚

I understood what the young lad was asking and what most of the people in the audience really wanted to ask. Why? Because just a few years before, that was the question Belinda and I also were asking. For most of my life, I had been a "make-it-happen" kind of guy. You know the type. Make a plan. Work the plan. Bask in your success. Then make another plan, and repeat the process ad infinitum—or is it ad nauseum? For a Type A personality like myself, I couldn't imagine another way to live— that is, until God began to create unrest in me and in my wife.

> "For most of my life, I had been a 'make-it-happen' kind of guy. You know the type. Make a plan. Work the plan. Bask in your success."
> —*Lonnie*

For me, this way of life began when I was a kid. I grew up poor in the heart of the Appalachian Mountains near Hazard, Kentucky. In my family, whatever we had we worked hard to get. We worked hard all summer growing a garden and canning the produce in order to eat all winter. We worked hard for any "extras." I sold the *Grit* newspaper. (*Grit* was a national paper that young people, typically males, sold door to door to earn extra money and receive prizes. I sold enough to earn my first pocket knife, which was called a "Grit Knife," of course.) Regularly, my brother and I went into the hills and cut felled trees into kindling and sold the kindling for ten cents a bushel. I also often worked in my Uncle Arkansas Riley's gas station (we called it a "filling station"), pumping gas, filling jars with motor oil, and stocking shelves.

He didn't pay me for my work, but he did give me my fill of soda (we called it "pop"), candy, and other items from the store.

Not only did I apply my "can-do" method to earning money, but I also applied it to other things I wanted to achieve. I remember well how I handled the fact that I was too short to make the high school basketball team. Instead of giving up and settling for something else, I set my mind on playing basketball. In the winter, when all the other boys in town were out sledding, I practiced ball day after day after day. I didn't make the high school team, but I did make the team in college. And I did so well that I made the local newspaper after scoring twenty-three points in one game. I had arrived! I took the newspaper clipping to my high school coach, who by then was a college coach, showed him what I had done, and said, "Now, tell me I can't play." I had set a goal, devised a strategy, and made it happen. I was proud of my achievement.

All that was well and good, for it taught me the value of a dollar and the value of hard work. But the downside was that it also taught me that if I got my strategy right and worked my plan hard, I would get the results I wanted. It taught me that *I* could "make it happen."

Unfortunately, when I became a Christian in college, I took that same method into my walk with the Lord. I was never taught any other way. Looking back, I realize that it was the common thought among Christians as the way to achieve the American Dream. I never once thought I could earn my salvation; I knew it was a free gift of grace from a loving God. I knew it was made possible only through the sacrificial death of His Son Jesus on the cross. In my mind, that was settled. But the model for how to live the Christ-life was taken from business, not from the Bible. And, unfortunately, that was the model most Christians were being taught. It was "plan the work, work the plan, and you will be successful."

And so I planned and I executed my plan. I completed a two-year college program in civil engineering. In April 1970, I married a wonderful Christian girl from Lynch named Belinda Brummitt. We headed north to Ohio, our plan underway to get out of the mountains as soon as possible. We started our family. We got involved in a local church, satisfied to be active laypeople. All seemed to be going well.

We planned our life, and we worked our plan to be successful at everything we attempted. I had a good job. We purchased our first home. Our children—Lisa, Brian, and Amy—were happy. We were content to teach Sunday school, drive our church's bus to bring people to church, and continue on the path to achieving the American Dream.

During that time, I also did some lay preaching, which led to a church in a racially changing West Dayton, Ohio, community asking if I would be interested in becoming pastor. I agreed. True to form, I wanted to be the best pastor I could be, so I put my basketball skills to work and joined in on every parking lot game I saw. Soon many of those basketball-playing young men began coming to church. And then, they began bringing their families. When church attendance reached 120, I felt overwhelmed and had no idea what to do next. I talked with several people who suggested that I needed more education, and so after two years in Dayton, we headed back to school.

With pastoral ministry as our new goal, we moved back to Kentucky for me to pursue a bachelor's degree in religion at Cumberland College (now University of the Cumberlands) in Williamsburg. We arrived with our truckload of belongings and our three children, but with no place to live and no job. Very late on our first day in Williamsburg, my brother found a small mobile home in which we could live. After about six weeks, God provided a church for me to pastor, a house for our family, and a job for Belinda as well.

For Belinda, those years were very fulfilling. She enjoyed campus life. She enjoyed her full-time job. She enjoyed being a pastor's wife even though she had resisted the pastor's wife idea initially. She enjoyed being a mom. She also took classes at the college to improve her secretarial skills. When a college counselor suggested she pursue a degree in business, she began work on that, too. And as with everything else, she excelled, making all A's. Little did she know that many years later in Lynch, those business and accounting skills would be put to great use in the ministry.

Of those years, Belinda says, "I wanted to be a good pastor's wife, so I stretched myself to study, and God blessed those efforts. Looking back, however, I see that most of what I did was performance-based. I read and I studied and I prayed, but I did not watch for or connect with what God was doing. He certainly took care of me in my ignorance. I prayed and I knew that God was directing our paths, but I did not know to watch everyday to see God at work."

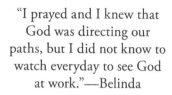

> "I prayed and I knew that God was directing our paths, but I did not know to watch everyday to see God at work."—Belinda

During my last two years in college, I also was an assistant to the president of the college. In that role, my drive to succeed continued. Not long after I had been hired, the president asked me to assume the responsibility of planning and conducting a conference for area pastors. It seemed the school had offered one such conference and spent a lot of money on it, but only six people attended. The president asked if I could "fix it." I said I would think about it and get back to him. And then, "make-it-happen" set in. Sure I could "fix it." And I did. I started with a list of sixty men, and at the first conference, forty men plus their wives and children showed up—one hundred people in all. I felt it was a great success. I had planned the work and worked the plan. I would never have thought to ask, "Did God do it or did Lonnie do it?" So, I was on to bigger and better things.

After that first conference, I set up a Church Advisory Board to plan the annual conference. Each year, the attendance grew. Thirty-two years after that first successful meeting, the conference is still going strong with approximately 160 pastors attending each year.

During the second year that I was on the college staff I traveled to Ohio to represent the school at a meeting of Southern Baptists from across that state. As I watched and listened to a parade of well-known preachers from across the Southern Baptist Convention preach that week I thought, "I'm going to be on that stage soon." And soon, I was. A year later, not only was I there, but I was running the program.

---

In 1981, Belinda and I and our three children moved to Columbus, Ohio, when I became assistant director of evangelism for the State Convention of Baptists in Ohio. We were on our way up the denominational ladder. Soon thereafter, my boss, the convention's executive director, asked me to organize a program that would reach two thousand youth. I said I would if he would give me three things: the freedom to do the program the way I wanted, the freedom to secure program personnel who would attract youth, and a budget that would allow me to get the job done. I don't remember saying anything about seeking God's will and what He wanted. My boss agreed and I set to work. *SAM* was my plan: make those goals *Specific, Attainable, Measurable* and I would be successful—and I would have the statistics to prove it.

At the time I came on board, about four hundred youth from twenty local associations of churches across the state were involved in the program. "No problem to fix that," I thought. "Just get each association to bring fifty kids to each event. Doable. *Specific. Attainable. Measureable.*" And it worked. The next year, attendance at the Ohio Baptist Youth Evangelism Conference jumped from four hundred to

"What I could visualize was what I attained. God was in it as far as I knew to let Him be. What would God have done if I had let Him be God and had not limited Him to what I could do?" —*Lonnie*

6

two thousand. So I set new, higher goals. By the seventh year, about six thousand were attending each year.

Today, I look back and think that in a state of fourteen million people, six thousand wasn't much to brag about. And I wonder what would have happened if I had known to let God show me what He wanted to do to reach the masses. What I could visualize was what I attained. God was in it as far as I knew to let Him be. What would God have done if I had let Him be God and had not limited Him to what I could do?

———

The die was cast. I was a performer who could make things happen. Because of my ego and my Type A personality, I was never threatened by anyone. My models became those ministers whom I considered to be successful. I began to compare myself to others with my same calling and began to compete with them to become as good as or better than they were at their jobs. As for those ministers and laypersons who lived by faith, thankfully, I was never turned off by them. Instead, I just didn't think it was possible for Belinda and me to live like they did. With my "make-in-happen" mentality, which Belinda also bought into, if I could have figured out how they lived by faith, I would have done it. But neither Belinda nor I could figure it out.

During our years on the Ohio convention staff, we had plenty of opportunities to rub shoulders with people who had figured it out. Men such as Manley Beasley, Vance Havner, and Jack Taylor. Men such as Junior Hill and R.G. Lee. Women such as Marolyn Ford and Joni Erikson Tada. When they spoke at our meetings, they told stories about how they would sense an urging from God to go to a certain city to preach but would have no money to buy a plane ticket. By faith, they would go to the airport, get in line, and before they reached the ticket desk, someone behind them would tap them on the shoulder and say, "Excuse me. I have this extra ticket that I can't use. Could you use it?" They told how God had brought sweeping revivals without their orchestrating them. They told how God had provided resources for their ministries. All these were wonderful stories, but foreign to our experience.

Often, we were asked to host these men and women, and we would use the opportunity to pepper them with questions about what they had shared in the meetings. Afterward, we would ask, "Can the things they talked about really happen to people?" I would ask Belinda if she really believed that the things they were telling were true. And she would always reply, "Yes. It's in the Bible." We would pray like we thought these great men and women of God prayed; God wouldn't show up for us; and we would swing back into our SAM mode where we were comfortable. Yet, somehow we both held on to the dream that what these men and women taught could happen to us although we really didn't think it ever would. We thought faith was a theory to be lived out by the spiritual elite; it was not for us. Even when we preached about faith and taught about faith, it wasn't really about faith; it was about what *we* could do.

Looking back, perhaps we didn't "get it" then because we were in the middle of "successful" activities and we were popular. We wanted to live as "successful" people lived and really didn't see the need for anything different. Little did we know, however, that God was developing a thirst in us that would not be quenched until we, too, surrendered our all—our dreams, goals, and ambitions to the Father— and yielded to His leading.

Looking back, perhaps we didn't "get it" then because we were in the middle of "successful" activities and we were popular. We wanted to live as "successful" people lived and really didn't see the need for anything different.

8

After spending seven years on the convention staff, in 1988 I left to become pastor of a church in southern Ohio. There I continued to be a "make-it-happen," SAM minister. In fact, the heading on the memo pads on which I wrote notes to my staff said "A Make-It-Happen-Line from Lonnie." Not only did I continue to live by that motto, but I expected everyone else around me to buy into it also. My goal was to be the pastor of a successful church with a big budget, big buildings, and big evangelism numbers. My goal was to be somebody and to be noticed.

For a while, everything was perfect. We even had the statistics to prove our success as the church grew to be the third largest in the Ohio convention. We were constantly busy, promoting the next program or planning the next big event. It was all about doing the things necessary to be bigger and better. That was all we knew to do. Everything was perfect—until we experienced the first major crisis of our lives. I was forty years old and Belinda was thirty-eight.

Problems developed in the church. We faced a split as a staff member took twenty-five people and left the church. For the first time in our lives, we had to focus on the possibility of failure as there seemed to be a subtle rebellion among the staff. For the first time, they wouldn't complete those "make-it-happen" tasks I assigned. There Belinda and I were in a "successful" church, very confident that we could make anything happen; instead, all the things that we had made happen seemed to be falling apart. "How could this be?" we wondered.

I must admit that my own ego played a huge role. I was where I wanted to be, and I pushed everyone really hard. I had heard others say, "Lead, follow, or get out of the way," and that sounded good to me. Then other staff members and other church members began to leave. Inwardly, I was horrified, but I put up a good front and dealt with each devastating issue that arose. Belinda and I still thought we could "make it happen." Looking back, we realize that God was taking us to the lowest point in our ministry. He was getting us ready for something we could never have imagined.

And then came problems in our family. Our three children began to rebel and become involved in worldly things in the community. They began to live in ways that were inconsistent with what we had taught them. We were devastated.

Put plainly, when these crises hit, we were worn out. We were spent from living twenty years in the performance mode. Even for self-confident, self-assured people, there are always peaks and valleys in the "make-it-happen" mode, and both Belinda and I had experienced them. The peaks come when you are doing better than those whom you admire; the valleys come when you are doing worse.

> Plainly put, when crises hit, we were worn out. We were spent from living twenty years in the performance mode.

And now, for the first time in our ministry, we were "doing worse" and were worn down from failure. We were worn out from the strain in our family. In fact, I was so worn out that I decided it was time to quit the ministry and go back to engineering. I even went so far as to write my resignation letter, prepare a resume, and go to the 1991 annual meeting of Ohio Baptists, telling God that if nothing happened at that meeting to change my mind, I would go back to engineering, make some money, and live the good life.

As for Belinda, she was scared. She was tired of her stomach being tied in knots. She wanted the Lord to speak clearly about what we were to do. "It's amazing. When you go through times like that, you don't remember eating, sleeping, or what you did," she says. "You simply go through the motions of life, and your brain is somewhere else. I thought

Lonnie would resign after he returned from the meeting, so I was preparing myself for another move. I didn't know where, but true to fashion, I was preparing myself to handle anything."

God knew the mess we were in, and He was waiting for us. At the meeting, we spent some time with Henry Blackaby, who was the keynote speaker. His book, *Experiencing God*, was all the buzz that year. His stories brought back memories of similar stories we had heard in previous years, and once again the hunger for the faith-life was awakened in us.

And then something only God could have orchestrated happened. When a pastor friend who was hosting Blackaby had to attend an unscheduled meeting, he asked us to take Blackaby back to his hotel. We peppered him with questions all the way. We told him what was going on in our lives, and for forty-five minutes he preached to us. "Your focus is wrong," he told us. "Your focus is on yourself." I kept talking about *strategies* to walk with God and see Him do great things, and he kept talking about *God*. I wanted to know if there was something Belinda and I could do that God would bless and accomplish for us. Blackaby wanted us to know God.

After we got back home from the meeting, I was so distraught that I spent three days on the floor of my office, crying, reading Scripture, and praying. Belinda knew the seriousness of my despair and carefully guarded my privacy during those three days. God was merciful and heard my cries. He told me, "I want to show you *you* so that you can see *Me*." What He showed me was not pretty. I saw the pride, jealousy, envy, and hatred that I didn't even know I had. I confessed my sin, and God

> "I kept talking about *strategies* to walk with God and see Him do great things, and he kept talking about *God*. I wanted to know if there was something Belinda and I could do that God would bless and accomplish for us. Blackaby wanted us to know God." —*Lonnie*

changed me. Seeing myself as God saw me was the first step to true repentance, not just the kind where we give God a shallow "Forgive-me, I-won't-do-it-again" nod to repenting, but repentance that brings a radical forgiveness and a radical reversal in action and lifestyle.

For Belinda, the process of repentance and turning to God alone had already begun before our time with Blackaby. By the time we talked with him, she was already so broken by the crises we had faced that she was ready to trust. She simply cried out to God from the depths of her being, "Lord, I want to see You."

Belinda, our daughter Amy, and I immediately began studying *Experiencing God* together and began to experience what it means to have a personal relationship with God. Belinda describes this as "a fresh touch, when you are at your lowest and your inner being calls out to God." For her, the results were immediate. "My focus, my desire was Jesus. I wanted the Spirit so to fill me that when others were in my presence, they would see Jesus," she says. This was a major change for both of us. Belinda and I had "done" our daily devotions from the time we had become Christians, but we had never really experienced an intimate, personal relationship with the Father. In fact, it had been only a few years earlier that Belinda had first heard the words "a personal relationship with God." This was new territory for both of us.

Just a few days after meeting Blackaby, another defining "only-God-could-do-this" moment occurred for Belinda. In 1989, she and a friend had begun a house cleaning service, so it wasn't unusual to find her

"My focus, my desire was Jesus. I wanted the Spirit so to fill me that when others were in my presence, they would see Jesus."—*Belinda*

on her knees cleaning. But on that Thursday in November 1991, what happened while she was on her knees was unusual. That day, God spoke to her and told her to give up the cleaning service. She was stunned and visibly shaken. She did not tell her partner that day, but she did tell me that night. When she asked me what she should do, I told her to ask God, since He was the One who had told her to quit. That settled it for her. She felt she had no choice, since it had been such a compelling command. The next day, Friday, Belinda told her partner she was quitting, and they cried together.

The following day, Saturday, Belinda learned why she had to give up the business when her mother called from Kentucky with devastating news. She was losing her eyesight and needed Belinda to come help her. By Sunday afternoon, Belinda was on her way to Lynch, Kentucky, to care for her mom. Although hearing so clearly from God was a new experience for Belinda, she knew she had heard a sure word from Him, and she was ready to obey. She spent the next two weeks preparing to move her mom to Ohio to live with us. Our children and I joined them for our last Thanksgiving in the old homeplace, and then Belinda's mom moved in with us.

~~~

Needless to say, I didn't resign as pastor. My leadership style, however, did change dramatically. No longer was I program-driven and goal-oriented. I began to teach the people the ways of God and help them interpret their circumstances in light of those ways. I began to watch for how God was working. A hint of opposition did continue in the church, but nothing like the previous level. I remember one man who told me, "One thing I know: you have been with God." For Belinda and me, this entire experience set in motion a zeal to experience God that has continued uninterrupted until this day.

God was up to something new in our lives and Belinda and I were excited. We were learning that He was not finished with us. He began to do amazing things, things we had not experienced previously.

> God was up to something new in our lives and Belinda and I were excited. We were learning that He was not finished with us yet.

~~~

For example, one day after a Sunday worship service, a man asked to speak with me as soon as possible. I suggested the following Tuesday or Thursday, but he insisted that he needed to talk with me that very day. That afternoon, he told me he had a dreadful fear of dying. It was so strong that he would not hold his small son on his chest for fear the child would break the father's ribs, and his heart would stop beating. But the deeper fear was that he would die and spend eternity without God. That day, as we prayed, he made peace with God. In my "make-it-happen" days, I would have checked my calendar and flatly told the man that I could not see him that afternoon and that he would have to make an appointment for later in the week. I would have missed the hand of God in his life and in mine.

One Sunday morning, I was surprised to see fifteen Russians in the worship service. I didn't even know there were Russians in our town, but God did. After the service, the woman who had brought the Russians told me she had invited a Russian woman with whom she worked, and that woman had invited the others. Then she asked, "Well, what am I to do?" When I asked her what the group had asked her to do, she said they hadn't asked her to do anything. So this is what I told her: "You don't do anything until they ask you to. Then you will know what to do." I was learning to wait on God, not jump in and devise a strategy.

The next Sunday morning, thirty Russians came. That day, the church member asked me, "Preacher, what do I do now?" I replied, "What have they asked you to do?" She replied, "They have asked me to start a Bible study in the neighborhood where they live." I replied, "Then you go teach them the Gospel of John. Teach them about Jesus." And she did.

From that group came two Russian congregations in Ohio. Several members of our church also traveled to Russia to build a church building for a congregation whose membership now numbers more than three thousand people. Because of those Russians, our senior adults got interested in their world and eventually sent Bibles to five continents.

God was showing us how to get in on what He was doing, not create our ideas of what He ought to be doing. And He was moving us out of our narrow world into His larger world.

These, however, were not the final nor the most difficult lessons Belinda and I needed to learn during those years. In 1993, the worst crisis of all hit our family; thankfully, through the previous crises, God had been preparing us to face this one. Had we not already begun to learn how to rely on God, we would not have made it.

That year, our nineteen-year-old-year-old son, Brian, was in a terrible auto accident and almost died. Sometime during that fateful night, Brian and a friend had wrecked their car, but it was hours before anyone came on the scene. In the middle of the night, Belinda answered our phone to hear a police officer inquire if she were a certain person. She kept asking the policeman questions until he finally told her that a young male at an accident scene had given the Riley phone number, but not the Riley name. The police needed someone to come to the hospital to identify the young man. I headed to the hospital. The young man was our Brian.

After a seemingly endless day of tests, we were told Brian would not live. He had a skull fracture and seriously shattered vertebrae that had left him paralyzed from the chest down. When we finally were allowed to see him, he was plugged up to life support, and a hook was hanging from the ceiling to support his head to keep it off his neck. To see him like that was devastating. We were traumatized. "Oh, God, help our child" was all we could pray. Then we prayed, "Lord, help us to accept Your will." Later that night, we were summoned to Brian's side to be with him when he died. His blood pressure had bottomed out, and all signs showed that he was leaving us. But he did not leave us. A miracle occurred. During those long night hours, he began to improve.

15

The next day, Brian went to surgery, but when the surgery was completed, the doctors told us he would never walk again. We began our plans to make our home wheelchair-accessible.

Then another miracle occurred. After seven weeks of therapy to teach Brian how to live with his handicap, his hip snapped into place—and he began to feel pain. He was in therapy for about a year. It was worth all the time and energy required to care for him at home that year as, by the grace of God, to this day, Brian can walk. Unfortunately, the pain he experienced after the accident led him to begin using prescription drugs, which led to a long-term dependence on drugs that has continued to affect our family until this day.

It was indeed a frightening time for our family and yet there were moments when God's voice was clear. One word from God came through our sixteen-year-old daughter, Amy, as she stood by her brother's bedside and prayed, "Lord, even if You don't spare Brian's life, it's not going to change how I feel about You." She was learning to lean on God in every circumstance, and she was teaching us how to as well.

> "Lord, even if You don't spare Brian's life, it's not going to change how I feel about You."—Amy

Belinda and I expected to stay at that Ohio church for a long time, but God had other plans. In 1994, as we were leading a Bible study in the home of one of the couples in the church, He gave us both a Scripture that would set the course for the next phase of our lives: "You have dwelt long enough at this mountain. Turn and take your journey and go ... south" (Deuteronomy 1:6-7). Belinda asked, "What do we do with this?" I replied, "I don't know, but if it's the truth, God will have to show us." And He did.

In 1995, we went south—to a church in Mississippi, just outside Memphis. We moved from the third largest church in the Ohio convention to a church with less than 100 in attendance—and we knew that God was in the move. No longer were Belinda and I looking for "bigger and better." No longer did we need power, prestige, or position. No longer did the size of the congregation matter. All that mattered was that now God was personalizing His word for us. All that mattered was the desire of the people to see God. We now were looking for a people who were hungry to follow God as He would lead. We wanted to be a pastor and wife who would love the people, help them heal their wounds, and help them trust God again.

We moved to Mississippi with one prayer in our hearts: "Lord, teach us Your ways in order that we may walk in them. And strengthen us to teach these new friends the same."

In Ohio, we had lived in a nice older four-bedroom parsonage. We did not expect to have as much from the church in Mississippi, but God surprised us. For years, Belinda had carried a picture that she had clipped from a magazine of a large Tudor home; it was her dream home. As we were packing for the move, God told Belinda that He was going to give us her dream home. And He did.

God gave her that house when the church sold its building and parsonage and gave us the money to make a down payment on a five-bedroom, three-bath executive estate home near a forty-acre lake. It didn't take long for us to learn that the house was not ours, but God's. Out of the blue, pastor-friends began calling to ask if they could bring their families to visit us. When they would arrive on our doorstep, we would soon learn that they were hurting badly. One weekend, we had twenty people staying with us. Through them, God was giving us a

> No longer were Belinda and I looking for "bigger and better." No longer did we need power, prestige, or position.

> He was also teaching us that what He would provide for us was not for our comfort but for extending His kingdom.

word not only about how we were to minister, but He was also teaching us that what He would provide for us was not for our comfort but for extending His kingdom. It was about Him, not us.

At the church, things began to turn around as we spent the first months just loving the people and preaching and teaching the Word. At one time, about eight hundred people had worshipped there, but the church had long-since fallen on hard times. The people had been hurt so badly that many of them would stand in line just to receive a hug. When they began to heal, they were once again ready to launch out in ministry. Soon the congregation grew to four hundred in attendance. The church constructed a building valued at $3.7 million and moved into it almost debt-free. We began an Hispanic ministry/church in a nearby mobile home park, an African-American ministry, and sent short-term volunteer missionaries to five countries.

God was doing a great work. God was teaching us how to receive and release, receive and release, receive and release. He was rebuilding the church on the principles of faith He was teaching us.

<hr />

Life in Mississippi suited us just fine. The church was growing. We were learning to live by faith. Plus, we had a really great lifestyle. A five-bedroom Tudor estate home in a gated community near a forty-acre lake. A bass boat. ("Preacher, you live on a lake and don't have a boat?" one of the men of the church had asked. "I'll have to fix that." And he did.) Luxury cars. Cell phones provided by the church. Anything we wanted. Plus, a ministry to hurting pastors and families. Belinda and I both thought we would stay there until we retired. It was truly the "Life of Riley."

But, once again God had other plans, which he began to show us when Belinda's mother died in 1997 and we went back to Lynch for the funeral. While there, many people stopped by her home on Main Street to pay their respects. To tell the truth, through the years when we had gone back to visit Belinda's mother, we had pretty much stayed to ourselves. We thought the whole town was horrible and depressing, and we were always glad to get out of there and on our way back to the good life. We thought of Lynch as merely "the place where Mom lives."

This time, however, as people came by to visit, we began to change. God began planting seeds in us that would take a while to sprout, but when they did sprout, what plants they became for His glory! Several people who stopped by told us that we should move back home. They said things such as "You're a minister, aren't you? We need people like you to come and help us."

That kind of interaction had never happened before on any of our visits home, mainly because we had been so reclusive. This time, when people asked those questions, my response was what I now call the "standard Christian response." I said, "You're right. You need people to come and help, and we're going to pray for God to send them." You know how it is: we say we'll pray, but we don't intend to; we just want to get rid of folks and get on with our business.

We went back to Mississippi and thought no more about it; I'm not sure we even prayed for the folks. Another year passed before we had to return to Lynch to take care of mom's house. We had not been able to sell it, and a potential renter had fallen through, so we had decisions to make.

Once again, people stopped by. And when they did, several asked why we had not moved back home. God was still planting seeds in our hearts.

This time, we began to listen. As we drove around the town, it was as if we were seeing it for the first time. It's like seeing a crooked picture in your home. You see it at first, and then you don't. Then, one day, you do. This time we saw the houses that had sat empty

As we drove around the town, it was if we were seeing it for the first time.

19

for twenty years. This time we saw the poverty and the hopelessness. We saw the depth of hurt in people's eyes.

This time, as we made the ten-hour trip back to Mississippi we weren't thinking about returning to our comfortable lifestyle in what seemed to be a perfect setting for the culmination of a successful ministry career. This time, we were thinking about the people of Lynch, Kentucky. *Our* people.

Before long, we were both in tears. Simultaneously and independent of each other, on that long drive south, we both came to the realization that we were to move back home. We knew we were to leave our affluent church, our almost six-figure salary, our dream home, and our expensive cars and move to the mountains to live in the little four-room duplex where Belinda had grown up. We did not question; we did not doubt; we knew what we had to do. When God spoke to us, it was a done deal. That experience with God was so awesome that it almost took our breath away.

Over the next months, confirmation came as we studied Scripture. Isaiah 41:17-18 became precious to us: "The poor and the needy are thirsty, and there is no water. But I, the God of heaven, have heard them. I will make a river to flow from the mountains so that all men will know that God has done this thing." (Lonnie's paraphrase)

———

That trip to Lynch and that call of God had come in November, but we waited to tell our family and to resign until January 1 so that we could be with our family and the people of the church through the Christmas season. Then we sold our home and gave the money back to the church, because the church had loaned it to us in the first place. We turned in our leased cars. We gave our daughter and son-in-law our boat. On March 1, 1999, we headed to Lynch.

Looking back, the first sign that God would provide for us came in the move itself. Five years earlier, the tab for our move from Ohio to Mississippi had been seven thousand dollars, which had been paid for by the church. This time, we would be personally footing the bill. Then God intervened. In Mississippi, I also had a horse, which I was boarding at a riding club. One day I met a man who had recently begun boarding his horse at the same facility. As we talked, I learned that he, too, was a believer. Later, I told him about what God was doing in our move to Appalachia. He seemed somewhat surprised, but then he said he owned a moving van line and offered to move us to Lynch for just the cost of the fuel. I knew God had placed him in that riding club for a divine purpose.

And so we arrived in Lynch without a job, without income, and with no clue as to how we would support ourselves. (We thought we had enough money to live on for about a year.) We, however, arrived with something more precious than jobs or income. We arrived with the absolute certainty that we were in

The word from God to us was this: "You won't have a fancy house, cars, or boat. You won't even have a salary. But you will have Me."

the place God wanted us to be and that He would take care of the details. The word from God to us was this: "You won't have a fancy house, cars, or a boat. You won't even have a salary. But you will have Me." Our response was, "If we have You, that's enough."

We arrived in Lynch, ready to trust God and listen for what He wanted us to do next. We prayed. And we waited for a new word from Him.

# TWO

$\sim$

# "NO NEW WORD FROM GOD"

*We* arrived in Lynch at midnight on a cold March night ready, willing, and eager to hear from God about what we were to do. God had dramatically interrupted our lives and redirected us onto a whole new course with Him. God had changed our thinking and our circumstances. This movement of God in our lives not only put us on a different life course, but more importantly, it set us on a journey with God that was to be characterized by faith.

We now call such an encounter with God a "radical intersection." For some people, such an intersection is a single, spectacular encounter with God that occurs in a moment; for others, it is a brief season of life. Either way, God leads us to a defining moment that requires a faith response. And when we respond in the affirmative, it does not mean we become perfect, smarter, richer, or immune to failure. It does not mean we become spiritual giants. It simply means that we will have the phenomenal joy of experiencing the presence and power of God as He does things through our lives that only He can do.

But when Belinda and I arrived in Lynch, we really had few clues about all that. Perhaps we thought God would give us a word as to what to do next that would be as strong and obvious and plain as the word He had given us on that trip back to Mississippi after we had been in Lynch to settle Belinda's mother's affairs. Perhaps we expected a continuing, immediate response so we would know exactly what to do next.

And so we waited. But no new word came. We waited, and waited, and waited, but for six months, we heard no new word from God. For six months, it seemed that in our situation He was saying nothing and doing nothing.

What do you do when you have obeyed God's call, resigned from your job, packed up and moved, and then don't have a clue as to what to do next? You wait on God. You learn that waiting is God's way of bringing you to a greater understanding of how He works. You begin to listen and to look at your surroundings with fresh eyes. You begin to look for God to show up in the ordinary. Most importantly, you just hold on to the last thing God told you, because when God tells you something, it doesn't matter if it takes six months or six years or sixty years, He's going to do it. When God says it, it's as good as done. You begin to learn what it means to make a faith response to what He *has* revealed. You begin to learn what it means that God alone is enough.

> What do you do when you have obeyed God's call, resigned from your job, packed up and moved, and then don't have a clue as to what to do next? You wait on God.

So for those six months as we waited, Belinda and I worked on Mom's four-room coal-town duplex. Ironically, we never actually moved into that house. Instead, we turned it into a guest house for visiting family and friends. We bought the house next door, moved into it, and with the help of volunteers, renovated it over the next five years.

We also walked the streets of our town and tried to absorb what we saw. Everywhere we went, we saw boarded-up houses. We saw an empty recreation field. We saw a closed hospital. We learned that absentee landlords owned about 90 percent of the land. We learned that the unemployment rate was nearly 50 percent. We learned that the adult illiteracy rate was also nearly 50 percent. And most disturbing of all, we saw a church that had closed a few months before—the church in which we both had been baptized, in which we had been married, and in which I had preached my first sermon. And this time as we walked around Lynch, we took it all in; God had opened our eyes.

Really seeing the state of her hometown was especially difficult for Belinda since she remembered what Lynch had been like when she was growing up. At its peak in the 1920s, 30s, and 40s, the town had been home to more than ten thousand people representing thirty-eight nationalities as U.S. Steel had brought in immigrants from around the world to work in the coal mines. When the town was built by a subsidiary of U.S. Steel in 1917, the company had touted it as the world's largest coal camp and as a model company town, complete with company housing for its employees; company-provided health care, education, and churches; and company-sponsored cultural and educational events.

Even though the influence of coal had dwindled by the time Belinda came along, the town was still vibrant. "I remember the theatre where my friends and I went to the movies; the majestic hotel standing tall on the hillside; people walking around town day and night; our school winning four state football championships; doctors and nurses making house calls; groups of children playing outside almost anytime of the year; churches filled with people; and Saturday trips to the 'Big Store' in town where we could buy almost anything we wanted. I remember hearing about how in an earlier decade Count Basie's orchestra had played in our town. I also remember hearing about how more than twelve thousand spectators often joined in cheering for the town's semi-pro baseball team. I remember an *alive* town," she says.

Following the collapse of the coal industry and the lay-off of huge numbers of miners in 1959, many families moved away. Hundreds of houses were left vacant; many eventually were torn down. The Lynch mine closed in the 1960s. The town was eventually sold. It incorporated as a city in 1963.

Now, as we walked the streets and inspected the buildings, we saw homes, schools, and public structures in bad repair. Rusty plumbing, leaking roofs, sagging floors, faulty electrical wiring, and peeling paint on clapboard marked most buildings. Now, only about nine hundred people lived in Lynch. And only about fifteen thousand lived in the towns of Lynch, Benham, and Cumberland, which form the Tri-Cities. (Hemmed in by Black Mountain, the highest point in Kentucky, and Pine Mountain, the three towns flow into each other with only city signs to indicate where one town ends and another begins. The same "Main Street" runs the seven and a half miles from the beginning of Cumberland, through Benham, to the eastern end of Lynch. Lynch itself is approximately one hundred yards wide at its narrowest and three hundred yards wide at its widest. Benham, too, was a coal-company town and was owned by International Harvester.)

Now, we really looked at our street, the two-and-a-half-mile long section of Main Street that defines the boundaries of Lynch. On our street alone, there were thirteen empty houses, most of them framed by overgrown hedges. It looked like a jungle. We knew that we were to do something about what we saw. I said, "Well, God's called us here to help people, so the least I can do is make the town look better." I drove the thirty miles to the nearest big

On our street alone, there were thirteen empty houses, most of them framed by overgrown hedges. It looked like a jungle.

store and bought a set of hedge trimmers for $24.99. I also bought a one hundred-foot extension cord. Then I went up and down the street clipping the hedges in front of all those empty houses. Little did we know that in that simple act God would give His first words to us about how we were to live by faith.

During that spring of hedge-trimming, a young man stopped by our house and said something like this: "Somebody told me you are a preacher, and I really need help. I need seventy-five dollars. My kids are hungry, my car's torn up, and I can't get to work."

I had no reason to doubt the man's need because there were so many needy people in Lynch and no one just "passes through" Lynch looking for a handout. It's a seven-mile mountain crossing up one side and seven miles down the other side, so you have to be "going there" to get there. So I said to him, "Man, I don't have seventy-five dollars, but if God gives me seventy-five dollars, I'll know who it belongs to." I had learned to respond in that manner during our last days in Ohio when the part-time pastor of our church's mission congregation wanted to become full-time. Back then I had told him, "I don't have a dime to spare, but if God gives me one dime, I will give it to you."

Two days after the hedge-trimming experience, Belinda and I were in our back yard scraping paint off an old door when a woman pulled up in a Jeep with Ohio license plates. She got out of the vehicle, crossed her arms, and said, "I've come to pay my bill." I replied, "Ma'am, you don't owe me a bill that I know of. I don't even know who you are." She said, "I'm the owner of the empty house up the street three doors from you, and I was going to pay to have my hedges clipped like I always do. I am going to pay you because you did such a good job."

The woman then took out a one hundred dollar bill, placed it on the old door and said, "Now, if you don't pick up that hundred dollar bill, it will just lay there." Then she got in her car and drove off. Now, you don't say that to a broke preacher in Eastern Kentucky and not see action. I thought, "I'm going to Western Sizzlin over in Harlan tonight and get me a steak." (Don't worry. I was going to take Belinda, too.) I picked up the money and began to make plans to drive the thirty miles to the steak house. I could almost taste the steak.

But God got to me first. As I walked into our house, it was as if He said, "Lonnie, you remember that yesterday you told that boy that if I gave you seventy-five dollars, you'd give it to him. I just gave you more than seventy-five dollars." I immediately replied, "Lord, You are right."

You can't imagine the joy in my heart as I went inside and called the young man. "Listen, I just want you to know that God's been good to you today," I said. "I told you that if God gave me seventy-five dollars, I would give it to you. Well, God just gave me seventy-five dollars, and I'm going to give it to you. I just want you to know that when your family sits down tonight to a warm meal for the first time in a long time, and you are able to drive your car to work in the next few days, God has been extremely good to you."

As soon as I had hung up, I headed out the back door to deliver the money. Before I had gotten far, it was as if God touched me on the shoulder and spoke audibly to me. He said, "Now Lonnie, I just want you to know that not only did I give that boy the $75, but also I paid you back the $24.99 for your hedge clippers all in one shot."

Wow! I could hardly wait to tell Belinda what I was learning about waiting on a new word from God. As I look back, I now see that all waiting carries a test with it: will we take matters in our own hands (as the "old" Lonnie and Belinda would have done), or will we really wait on God? Waiting means we do not take into our hands what only God can do. God tests us to see if we are willing to make changes in our thinking that will result in our utter dependence on Him.

While a word from God is for us, it is not about us; it is always about the advancement of His kingdom.

As we look back, we see that God had started the process of

putting that pattern into our lives in Ohio. By the time we moved to Lynch we had begun to understand what hearing a word from God meant. While a word from God is *for* us, it is not *about* us; it is always about the advancement of His kingdom. And while a word *from* God is personal, it is always consistent with the Word *of* God as given in Scripture. Our task is to watch and wait and listen for a word from Him *before* we do anything. That is a clear pattern throughout Scripture. Look at Moses, for example. God's word to him to lead the Israelites out of bondage in Egypt was not about Moses; it was about God (Exodus 3-4). Or look at the Apostle Paul. God's word to him was not about him, but about how God wanted to use him to spread the good news of the gospel (Acts 9).

And what does God accomplish through our waiting? The most important thing is that, if we will let Him, He will make our hearts right with Him. If our hearts are out of tune, we won't do what He wants us to do no matter how many times or how loudly He speaks. So, in a time of waiting, God can soften our hearts so that when He does give a new word, we will respond with a resounding "Yes."

In a time of waiting, if we will let Him, God will lead us to surrender completely to His will. In a time of waiting, He will teach us how to release our dreams to Him.

In a time of waiting, God teaches us to differentiate between wants and needs. I am 100 percent convinced that if our hearts are right with Him, when we ask something of Him, He will give it every single time. But I am just as convinced that God will not give us what we think we want, but He will give us what we need to have a strong relationship with Him. In a time of waiting, God can

> In a time of waiting, God can reorient us to think "faith-fully" about His desires for us.

reorient us to think "faith-fully" about His desires for us. He can help us learn that it's not about us, but it's all about Him.

In a time of waiting, God matures our faith as we become more dependent on Him. God helps us understand what faith in Him really is. It is not faith in something; it is faith in Someone—God Himself. Faith is relational, not merely intellectual. God does not want us to have faith that something will happen; He wants us to have faith in Him, who will cause things to happen.

In a time of waiting, God grows our confidence in Him as we learn to rest in the assurance that what He has promised, He will bring to pass in His time and in His way.

In that process comes renewed strength. The prophet Isaiah put it this way: "They that wait upon the Lord shall renew their strength" (Isaiah 40:31).

In a time of waiting, God teaches us to pay attention to His activity and become more aware of how He is continually at work in the world. I often wonder if in my former life I would even have noticed how God provided the money to meet the young man's needs and then gave me the money for the hedge clippers to boot. Would I have been too busy "making things happen" to see the hand of God? Would I have slowed down long enough to recognize God at work or would I have been "on to another item on my agenda?" Waiting, I have learned, causes us to slow down and look for God at work.

In a time of waiting, God teaches us to act on what He places before us, no matter how insignificant those things may seem to be. Waiting is not inactivity; it often is opening our eyes to see what is at hand that needs to be done and then doing it.

In a time of waiting, God teaches us to act on what He places before us, no matter how insignificant those things may seem to be.

For me, doing what lay at hand was taking on those jungle-like hedges; for Belinda, it was reconnecting with her former classmates, teachers, and friends, many of whom were now leaders in the community. Although we had been gone for twenty-eight years, many remembered Belinda as the A student, cheerleader, and strong leader she had been in high school. God used her reputation as an entry point back into the community and as the power behind the strong ministry that developed. We didn't have to reestablish credibility; we just had to tap into what was already there.

For both of us, what lay at hand were socks and cookie dough.

A couple of weeks before our first Christmas back home, a local sock factory gave us thousands of socks. There, however, was a catch: the socks were seconds, and they were singles; there were no pairs in the lot. We piled them in our living room, and over the next several days Belinda, our son, and I spent every spare moment sizing and pairing them up. We jokingly said that the Christmas glitter in our home that year was not on the tree but in the plastic ties on the floor. When we had finished, we distributed all those socks. They kept a lot of feet warm that winter.

A week or so after we had finished the sock project Belinda walked out our back door to find a thirty-pound-box of cookie dough on the porch. Since it had already thawed, she knew the dough would have to be used promptly. Plus, Belinda, Brian, and I were leaving for the Christmas holidays in a few days, and we knew we would have to get those cookies baked before we left town. So, we did what was at hand: for two days, eight to ten hours each day, we baked cookies. We filled plate after plate with cookies, wrapped the plates, and tied them with pretty bows.

After we had finished, we spent the next two days delivering the cookies. On the first day, snow began falling; we felt we were in a Currier and Ives painting as we went down the streets of Lynch singing Christmas carols, knocking on doors, and giving cookies. Needless to say, folks were surprised and gladly received our gifts.

"But who left that dough on your porch?" you ask. To this day, we have no idea. All we *do* know is that God put that cookie dough there as a test to see if we were willing to use what was at hand for His glory.

As Belinda and I waited, we also began to pray more fervently. If we had a strategy, it went something like this: "Lord, You know more about Lynch and Harlan County than we do. We trust You to do what's right. Anytime You want to let us know what You are going to do, that's okay, too. You're God, but if You want us to get in on what is going to go on around here, just let us know what You want us to do." We would soon learn that is a key principle in living a life of faith. It's not about strategy but about serving. It's not about sacrifice but about surrender. It's not about trying but about trusting. Caution: When a person prays that prayer and really means it, he or she had better be ready for what is about to happen.

Four months after we moved back, Belinda and I were invited to attend a prayer meeting in the city park in a nearby town. We expected a handful of people to show up on that July day, but when we arrived, about 250 people from Lynch and the

> It's not about strategy but about serving. It's not about sacrifice but about surrender. It's not about trying but about trusting.

surrounding area had gathered. Amazingly, even though we had not been involved in the preparations for the meeting, one of the planners asked me what the people should pray for. I responded that we should first pray for forgiveness for relying on everything but God. I said that in the past we had relied on the coal mining industry and on the government and look where that had gotten us. I said we also should pray for the things that would help the quality of our lives honor God. I said that for many people, that would require a job; therefore, we should pray for jobs for the people in the area.

We will never forget what happened as people began to pray with a fervency that we have rarely ever experienced. They literally fell to the ground, weeping and pleading with God to restore their land. I can only describe their cries to God as "wailing" as they cried out, "God, could You return to us?" I've never heard such crying out to God publicly, before or since. We spread out around the park, joined hands, and prayed to God to return to us and forgive us for trusting in everything but Him. It was heart wrenching to know that people really desired to see God move in their lives and in their communities.

That day, we learned that for many years many Christians in the area had carried the same burden for the people of the mountains that we now had. We were humbled to know that once again God had gone before us to prepare the way. We were learning to live in the assurance that faith will not lead a person to any place that God has not already been.

That day, another thing that only God could have orchestrated happened. As I said, we had nothing to do with planning the prayer meeting and yet a television reporter asked to interview me and asked what the meeting was about. My response

> We were learning to live in the assurance that faith will not lead a person to any place that God has not already been.

was that it was about a community returning to God. That day, Belinda and I could never have imagined that the prayer meeting would provide the foundation for all God would do over the next years. It gave us focus and direction.

Each month that fall and early winter, God revealed another part of His plan. In August about five months after we had returned home to Lynch, the infrastructure for the ministries that would emerge over the next years began to unfold. Looking back, this was the new word from God for which we had been waiting.

That August, we attended a conference for leaders in our denomination who were working in the ten-state Appalachian Mountain region. In one of the break-out sessions, we were asked to describe our ministry. We just honestly said that we had no idea what we would be doing. (What a change for a former "make-it-happen" guy who in the "olden" days would have pulled out a long list of exactly what we would be doing and how we were going to accomplish it all. Indeed, God had performed a miracle in us.) We said we only knew that God had called us back to the mountains to help people. After the session, a man from Knoxville, Tennessee, approached us. He said he was the director of a newly formed group called Mission of Hope that had been set up to resource mountain ministries, and he offered to help us. He would become one of our strongest supporters for the next several years.

Also, about that time we received a packet of material from the missions team of our state denominational headquarters that contained information about people who had expressed interest in summer ministry projects in Appalachia. Being new to the system, we thought we were expected to contact each of them—and we did. We saw this as God's word about the next step we were to follow. When we talked to them by phone, we asked what they wanted to do. Some said they would like to repair homes; others said they wanted to lead vacation Bible schools. We said, "If God is calling you to come, then by all means, come ahead." We later learned that for several years more volunteers had been ready to serve in Eastern Kentucky than there were places for them to serve.

In September, God provided our first building. A woman in North Carolina called a man in Virginia who called a man in South Carolina who called a friend in Louisville, Kentucky, to say that the woman owned a building in Cumberland and that she was interested in making it available for ministry. As God would have it, the morning after our friend in Louisville received the call, Belinda and I were already scheduled to meet with him and several others in Louisville. That day, the woman in North Carolina made the building available for one dollar a year. It would become the Freedom Center, which for several months housed both our food and clothing ministries. In 2001, we purchased the building.

That fall, we also met with the Lynch City Council several times. We started talking about cleaning up the city park. We told the council that as soon as God gave us the word, we would take on the park project. That put us on the map with the city officials.

In December, Mission of Hope hosted a Christmas party for two hundred children in Lynch, which opened our eyes to an incredible need. When the children arrived on that winter day, we could hardly believe what we saw. Most were wearing shorts and short- sleeved garments. Many were barefoot. When we asked about this, we learned they had no winter clothing. We wondered if they would survive when the harsh mountain weather set in. (Later that winter, the wind chill factor hit thirty-four degrees below zero.) We began to pray something like this: "Lord, in the Bible we see that You provided everybody, even Adam and Eve, with some clothing. Surely You can provide these children with clothes. Surely You can give us clothing that we can give to folks in Jesus' name so that they might know of Your wonderful deeds and glorify You." We were learning to ask God for specific things that would glorify Him.

Also, throughout the latter months of 1999 and into early 2000, we began receiving calls from local residents asking us if we could help them with specific needs. We began a list of their requests, most of which were for home improvements or food or clothing. One call was particularly humbling. A woman simply asked, "Are you the people who help people?" At first, we hired a local unemployed couple to do the home repairs; then God began

> A woman simply asked, "Are you the people who help people?"

sending volunteers who asked to do the specific things the local people needed.

In May 2000, Belinda and I were asked to speak at a state-wide meeting of leaders in our denomination. On the four-hour drive to the meeting, we focused our thinking on the upcoming summer and decided to tally the number of people who had said they would be coming to Lynch to help. When Belinda pulled out her cardboard box "filing system" with all the bits and pieces of paper and began counting, we were in for a shock. More than six hundred people had committed to come, beginning the very next month! We had no idea we had said "Yes" to so many. But what could we have done? We certainly could not have turned anyone down, because we had recruited no one. We knew their commitments were responses to God's work in their lives. That would be the beginning of the more than thirty thousand volunteers from thirty-five states and four countries who would come to work in Lynch and the surrounding area in the next ten years.

Not another new word from God? Hardly. We were learning that when God seems silent, He is still active in our lives and in His world. We were learning that when we respond to the seemingly little things He sets before us, our faith increases and our walk with Him deepens.

> We were learning that when God seems silent, He is still active in our lives and in our world.

And that deeper walk is the greatest reward of faith. We were learning that when we respond in faith, He turns the seemingly little things into big things that bring glory to Himself and Himself alone. In a nutshell, we were learning that faith is not a leap into the dark, but a step into the light.

THREE

———

# "FAITH IS NOT A LEAP INTO THE DARK, BUT A STEP INTO THE LIGHT"

*"You* have to hear what the Lord said to me today." I could hardly contain my excitement when I phoned Belinda from the conference I was attending in North Carolina, but before I could tell her, she said, "But you first have to hear what He said to me today."

It was the summer of 1992, seven months after we had talked with Henry Blackaby, and we were in the midst of sorting out what we were learning about how to experience God's presence and power in our lives. That day, in Ohio, God had given Belinda Exodus 34:10: "Behold, I make a covenant. Before all your people I will do marvels such as have not been done in all the earth, nor in any nation. And all the people among whom you are shall see the work of the Lord. For it is a terrible thing that I will do with you." And that day in North Carolina, God had given me Isaiah 54:2: "Enlarge the place of your tent, and let them stretch out the curtains of your dwellings. Do not spare. Lengthen your cords, and strengthen your stakes."

In the years that followed, we learned that to follow the path on which those verses would lead us is not a leap into the dark of the unknown, as so many people think. Rather, it is a step into the light of experiencing God in all His fullness. We learned that faith is a step into the light of God's truth that leads to His fulfilling that truth in the lives of His children. It is not, as so many Christians believe, that we don't know what is going to happen, but we move forward anyway. That is presumption, not faith. It is that we *can* know what God is going to do *before* He does it. Of course, we cannot know all the details of how He will complete His promises, but *that* He will is never in doubt.

Later, in 1998, after we had moved to Mississippi, we received the promise of God in Isaiah 41:17, 20 that would be the word from Him that would set the direction for our ministry in Lynch: "The poor and needy seek water, but there is none; their tongues fail for thirst. I, the Lord, will hear them: I, the God of Israel, will not forsake them. I will open rivers in desolate heights, and fountains in the midst of the valleys; I will make the wilderness a pool of water. That they may see and know, and consider and understand together, that the hand of the Lord has done this."

As we continued to study Scripture, we came to see that when a person receives a promise from God, that is all the reality that is needed; for in the moment God promises, the promise becomes reality. In that moment a person possesses it in his or her heart, and in time the invisible will become visible. We found the promise in Hebrews 11:3 to be true: The invisible becomes visible even though no one else can see it.

> When a person receives a promise from God, that is all the reality that is needed; for in the moment God promises, the promise becomes reality.

Consider Abraham, for example. He didn't obey out of the blue. Instead, God showed him a truth, and that truth was that he was to go to a country to which he had never been before. Then God told him that He would make "a great nation" of him (Genesis 12:1-2). Abraham had to believe that God would really show up to lead him to that "unknown" country and give him descendants. In faith, Abraham set out for that "invisible" country, and because he did, he experienced what God had already told him would happen. He believed that what God had promised was already reality; then he experienced the "visible" truth of what he had believed. For Abraham, it was not a leap of faith into the dark. It was a step into the light of what he knew was already reality, because he trusted the character of God.

As for God's promise to Abraham that he would be the father of many nations and that his descendants would be too numerous to count, that too required his stepping out in faith into God's reality. He waited for a century before the "invisible" heir God had promised became "visible." (Genesis 21). Then a few short years later, God asked him to sacrifice that son of promise (Genesis 22). Abraham could have asked how it would be possible for God to fulfill His promise if Issac were dead, but instead Abraham lived in the surety of God's promise. The writer of Hebrews 11:19 gives a marvelous insight into Abraham's understanding of faith as a step into the light, not a leap into the dark. He writes that Abraham assumed God was going to raise Issac from the dead, because God had promised that Abraham would be the father of many nations and that promise could only be fulfilled through an *alive* Issac.

Or take Noah. Noah's step of faith did not occur *after* he experienced rain. It started when God said there would be rain, a natural phenomenon that many biblical scholars believe had never occurred before. It was Noah's knowledge of the truth of God's character that made his experience make sense. He believed, he obeyed God, and he built an ark. He then experienced the visible reality of the truth of what he believed: he was saved from the flood.

What, then, is faith? What is this step into the light? It is not getting a good idea and hoping it will come to pass. It is not a mystical idea for a select few. It is, however, the one response that God requires of every believer if He is to show Himself strong in his or her life. The writer of Hebrews says, "Without faith it is impossible to please God" (Hebrews 11:6). The word "impossible" implies that there isn't a fraction of a chance that pleasing God can happen without faith. Without faith, there isn't even a slight chance that your life or my life will please God. God has tied everything in our lives to our ability to walk by faith.

> Faith is the one response that God requires of every believer if He is to show Himself strong in his or her life.

What is faith? "Faith," says the writer of Hebrews, "is the substance of things hoped for, the evidence of things not seen" (Hebrews 11:1). What a rich definition! I remember asking a teen in Lynch what he thought of when he heard the word "substance." I thought he might say something about "substance abuse," but he surprised me. He said, "Stuff." That is a very good definition of the word "substance." Faith, then, is the "stuff, the content of, the makeup of, the essence of." And "hoped for?" In biblical terms, to "hope for" something is not wishful thinking. It is not to be clueless as to whether something will happen. Rather, it is to have confidence and assurance that what God has announced He will do, He will do. Then it becomes "evidence."

> Without faith, there isn't even a slight chance that your life or my life will please God. God has tied everything in our lives to our ability to walk by faith.

So, my paraphrase of Hebrews 11: 1 goes like this: "Faith is the stuff you're already convinced about and are sure of. And then it becomes evidence." Thus, to walk in faith is to live in the surety of the reality of all that God has promised, even though you haven't yet experienced it. It is to trust that the invisible is already reality and will be made visible in God's time.

A woman once said to me, "I sure would like to have as much faith as you have." That set me to studying what Scripture says about this. I saw that at the moment a person receives Jesus as Savior and Lord, he or she receives all the faith he or she is ever going to get.

But before I came to that understanding, God asked me a series of simple questions. "How much faith do I have?" He asked. The obvious answer is, "All faith." "Then," He asked, "Since I work through My Son and all I am resides in Him, how much faith does Jesus have?" Again, the obvious answer is, "All." God continued, "So, when a person receives Jesus as Savior and Lord, how much of Jesus does he or she receive?" Again, the obvious answer is, "All." He concluded, "So the conclusion is that because you receive all there is of Jesus and Jesus has *all* faith, then when you receive My Son, you receive all the faith you are ever going to receive." I came to see that the question is not how much faith do I have, but how much of Jesus' faith am I allowing Him to display through my life. That was a revolutionary thought for me.

Thus, as a believer, the woman who said she wanted as much faith as I have in fact already had as much faith as I have. We both have all of Jesus' faith. The question then becomes this: how much of Jesus' faith will she allow to work through her? The Apostle Paul puts it like this in Galatians 2:20: "I have been crucified with Christ: it is no longer I who live, but Christ lives in me; and the life which I now live in the flesh I live by faith in the Son of God, who loved me and gave Himself for me." Therefore, when someone looks at your life or my life, it isn't your faith or my faith they see, it is Jesus' faith. Again, the questions become: how much of His faith will I let work through me? How much of His faith will you let work through you?

Why is faith the one thing God requires of us? Because by placing our faith in Him, we are acknowledging that we need Him and that we need an ever-deepening relationship with Him. We know we need Him for salvation, but we have a more difficult time acknowledging that we need Him in the everydayness of our lives. Scripture says: "There is no other name [that is, Jesus] under heaven given among men by which we must be saved" (Acts 4:12). We often think that to talk of "faith" is to talk of a set of beliefs about God and nothing more. But Scripture also says that "we walk by faith" (2 Cor. 5:7).

Somehow we have missed the fact that faith is also defined as "walking in a relationship of confidence and trust in God." When the Apostle Paul said, "We walk by faith," he was referring to his lifestyle of trusting in God, not a set of beliefs. Of course, his walk by faith was grounded in a set of firm beliefs, but in this verse Paul was thinking about where his life had taken him and how he had placed his confidence in God every step of the way. He was thinking about how his faith had kept him connected with God, the source of his power.

Faith, then, not only is the first step required for becoming a Christian, but it is the fuel that keeps our relationship with God fresh and releases the power of God to work in our lives. Faith exercised leads to a deeper relationship with God. Faith keeps us close to Him.

> Faith, then, not only is the first step required for becoming a Christian, but it is the fuel that keeps our relationship with God fresh and releases the power of God to work in our lives.

After we have learned what faith is and why God requires faith, the next logical question becomes this: how does a believer make decisions based on faith? How can a believer know if a word is from God? The answer is simple: a word from God comes in the intersecting of need, the study of Scripture, and intense prayer. And a word from God always focuses on the needs of others, not on oneself.

Every person in the Bible who lived by faith had heard a word from God before he or she set out to meet a need. And every one was focused on others. Think again of Noah. He didn't build an ark until he heard a word from God, and he didn't build it for himself alone. And Moses? He just kept on tending sheep on the back side of the desert until God showed up with a word of direction for him to lead the people of Israel to deliverance (Exodus 3).

When people ask Belinda and me to help them make decisions about what they are to do next in their lives, we don't encourage them to change the way they are currently doing things if they indeed are sincerely living the Christ-life. Instead, we tell them they are already on the faith journey; therefore, the next step is to be sure their hearts and lives are clean before God; then they can begin to look for God to show up.

We point them to Moses, who kept on tending those smelly sheep until God showed up—and because Moses had been humbled and his heart had been made right with God, he recognized the presence of God at work in the unusual burning bush. We encourage people to look at the circumstances of their lives and begin to see God at work in the midst of those circumstances. Then, they will begin to see what God wants of them. We tell them, "If God gives you cookie dough (as He did Belinda and me that first Christmas we were back in Lynch), then make cookies."

Many of those with whom we have talked have caught the message. One young woman from South Carolina came to Lynch to cut hair for a few days at the Freedom Center. After she went back home and back to her work as a hair stylist, a client who was a former inmate at a nearby prison began talking about how female prisoners would love to have their hair cut and styled. At that moment, the hair stylist heard a word from God. She knew she was to go to the prison, cut and style prisoners' hair, and tell them about Jesus. And she did.

On another occasion, a young couple came to visit Lynch, saw God at work, and returned home to look for Him to show up in their lives. God led the man, who was a successful businessman, to begin a Bible study in his place of business. Not only did colleagues attend, but several customers also became regulars. In a very short time, ten men made professions of faith in Jesus as Savior. In the words of the young man, "After visiting Lynch, our definition of faith changed. In Lynch, God changed our lives."

Another couple told us that after a visit to Lynch, their relationship with God and with each other totally changed. Until the visit, they had never prayed together as a couple; after the visit, that changed. In Lynch, they heard a word from God and they obeyed.

Of course, not everyone who comes to Lynch "gets" the message of what the faith-life is all about. We just leave that with God.

When you hear a word from God and step into the light of the faith-life, it changes your world view. It changes the way you see things, the way you hear what people say, the way you feel about almost everything. Your actions begin to line up with the word from God, and you begin to see how God operates in His world. Then you want to get in on what He is doing.

> When you hear a word from God and step into the light of the faith-life, it changes your world view.

Over these last years, not only have Belinda and I learned many things about why faith is the one requirement God makes of us if His power is to be released in our lives, but we also have learned much about what it means to live in the confidence that we are walking into the light and not leaping into the dark. Several faith principles have emerged.

First, you can be sure that God is always ahead of you, lighting the way. Second, He always provides the right resources for the task at hand. Third, He always provides the right resources at the right time. Fourth, He always has your best interests at heart. We have seen these faith principals in action many times in our years in the mountains.

⟨⟨⟨

God *is* always ahead of you, lighting the way. He will not lead you to where He has not already been. He will not lead you down blind alleyways.

I remember when God brought a layman from Greensboro, North Carolina, to Lynch on a mission trip, but he soon learned the real reason for the trip was for him to deal with a call he had felt for two years to start a church in the Greensboro area. During those two years, he had talked with several ministers, but none had offered to help him. He came to Lynch, heard our story, and sensed God reminding him to begin a church. I asked him what, by that time, had become one of our standard questions: "What has God laid on your heart?" To my surprise, he replied, "God has told me to start a skateboard church. Now what am I supposed to do?"

I told him that if God was in it, He was already out in front of him. Therefore, he should look to see what God was doing already. I told him that he did not need to go out and do everything *for* God. Instead, he needed to watch to see what *God* would do, and then he would know what to do next. He returned home to watch and wait.

Not long after that, he called. "You won't believe what God did!" he said. "He gave us an indoor skating rink. We just had our first service with more than one hundred kids! Twenty of them came to know the Lord that night."

When that young man obeyed the call of God, he was not leaping into the dark of the unknown; rather, he was walking into the light where God already was at work, just waiting for him to show up. Faith was his coming to the realization that what God had laid on his heart two years before was already reality; he just couldn't see it. All along, God's provisions were in place, but the young man had to get in tune with what God wanted to do.

We often discuss this faith principle with people who are thinking about coming to be full-time volunteers in Lynch. Often, they want to know how they will get the money for their living expenses. They want to know how their health insurance will be paid. They want to know where they will live.

Those are very important, legitimate questions, but Belinda and I have learned not one of these is the most important question. The most important question is, "Do you believe God wants you to come to Lynch?" I usually answer their questions by telling them that if their concerns are all-consuming and they cannot release them to God, then they probably should not come to Lynch. But if they are willing to leave those things in the hands of God, then by all means come. I tell them if they do come, they will not be making a leap into the dark but taking a step into the light of the truth of how God relates to His people. For you see, God will not provide before we obey.

*God will not provide before we obey.*

Belinda and I have personally experienced God being out in front of us and providing the right resources at the right time many times since we have been back in Lynch. No experience has been more dramatic than what occurred about three years into our time back. It involved housing for volunteers.

The second summer we were back in Lynch, after we had made all those calls to potential volunteers during our first winter, six hundred volunteers came. The third summer, twelve hundred volunteers came; the fourth summer, two thousand. That was wonderful since those folks were making such a difference in the lives of so many people in Lynch and the neighboring communities.

The logistics, however, were a nightmare. Where do you house so many people in a town without motels or hotels? We put them in church basements and in abandoned homes. That was acceptable in our area, but we knew it was not the best, so we started praying that God would give us a mission house. We thought one big building to house volunteers comfortably would be ideal, but I'm not sure we had even considered how big the house would need to be.

As we began to pray about the need for housing for all those volunteers, I noticed an empty, twelve-room house down the street from where Belinda and I live. We thought it would be perfect for our needs, so we began praying that God would give us that specific house. We even thought about taking out a loan to pay for the house, but as we prayed, we didn't believe God was guiding us to go into debt.

We prayed intensely about that house for about two and a half years, but we lost it anyway. Someone else bought it! We thought we had somehow missed God's will.

A week after the house had sold, a volunteer came from Georgia to help us for a few days. While he was with us, he became interested in the abandoned four-story, ninety-five-room hospital in Lynch. It is one of the most historic buildings in town, a truly beautiful structure. Every stone had been carved by Italian masons hired by U.S. Steel in the early 1900s.

The man, who specialized in property renovation and resale, offered to buy the old hospital and lease it to us for one dollar a year for ten years to house our mission teams. Immediately we knew God was showing us that He wanted to give us a ninety-five-room house instead of a twelve-room house. (Looking back, a twelve-room house would barely have made a dent in our housing needs as the number of volunteers who came to Lynch continued to increase each year. God knew what was needed.)

I immediately tracked down the land company that owned the hospital, gave the contact information to the Georgia investor, and waited and prayed that God would do whatever He wanted to do.

We waited in the confidence of the reality of God's provision. Then three months later, things changed. A company representative called to say that the deal had fallen through and that the company planned to sell the hospital. I'll never forget what I said to him: "Man, don't do that! I believe that God wants to use that old hospital in the mountains for His glory." He asked me, "Do you really believe that?" I said, "Yes sir, I do." Then he said, "Then, why don't you buy it?" When I asked him what he wanted for it, he answered, "$85,000." I knew that was an incredible bargain, but I didn't even have $850. Still, I said, "Okay, I'll buy it."

When he asked how much money I had, I replied, "Oh, I don't have any money, but my Heavenly Father is rich, and when He gets ready He will buy this building." He laughed and said, "I know you're a man of faith, but the only thing I can do is to hold this for you for thirty days." I replied, "Well, that ought to be enough time for my Father to come up with that kind of money."

It would seem that would have been the opportune time to work the phones and write fund-raising letters, but Belinda and I did not do that. In fact, since we have been in Lynch we have never done fundraisers because we believe that if God is in something, it isn't our responsibility to "make it happen" by our own ingenuity. Instead, we did what we have always

We have never done fundraisers because we believe that if God is in something, it isn't our responsibility to "make it happen" by our own ingenuity.

48

done: we prayed and sent out the word to our prayer partners around the country, asking them to join us in praying that God would provide just what was needed. We prayed that He would provide a miracle. And He did. Over the next three weeks, we received twenty-five thousand dollars from various sources.

While we were praying about purchasing the hospital, a friend wanted me to go to the bank to get a loan. After telling him I did not sense that God wanted us to go into debt, I finally consented because of his insistence. In the meeting with a loan officer to discuss my finances, it became clear that I would not qualify. Because I don't receive a salary, I could not project my income for the coming year. After a lengthy discussion about how God was providing for Belinda and me, the loan officer declared, "Mr. Riley, I would love to help you, but I can't give you a loan based on that." I replied, "I'm so glad you said that! The only reason I'm here is so that my friend can know God's will for providing for the old hospital building."

(For the record, over the years in Lynch we have taken out loans. In fact, a year or so after the bank rejected our loan request to buy the hospital, the same bank gave us a loan to buy the Freedom Center. We have learned that sometimes God uses a bank, and sometimes He places individuals in our path through whom He wants to finance ministry.)

When the company agent called one week before the scheduled closing to ask me if I was ready to close, by all outward appearances I wasn't. But God had already signaled Belinda and me that He would provide, so I said, "Yes, sir, I am ready when you are." He said, "Okay, today's Tuesday. Next Tuesday at 1 p.m. will be your thirty days. Just bring the money. I'll have the deed, and we'll just exchange the deed and the money, and the building will be yours." I said, "Okay." I was learning that God is always ready.

Then he asked me, "How much money do you have?" I said, "I've got twenty-five thousand dollars." He replied, "Now you know you need eighty-five thousand dollars." I said, "Yes, but I don't need it today. You told me I have a whole week, right?"

You know the two faith principles we learned that day? Not only does God provide the right resources, but He is never late nor early; He's always on time. Only God knew that we would need to house as many as three thousand volunteers each summer, not six hundred—and He knew *when* we would need to house them and when we would need the money to buy the old hospital. It's so easy to want God to show up early so that we can figure out what to do with what He gives us, but He doesn't work that way. He works in His time and in His way, and what He does is always best.

> Not only does God provide the right resources, but He is never late nor early. He's always on time.

I went out of town the next day, which was Wednesday, confident that what God had promised was already reality. On Thursday, Belinda called to tell me that a man from Ohio had called to say he had been praying for us and felt impressed of the Lord to lend us some money for the purchase of the old hospital. I said, "Great, Baby, just tell him to send it on down. Whatever he doesn't send, we'll just pray for the rest. It's Thursday and we've got until next Tuesday, right? We're not going to worry about this. God's always on time." On Friday, when I called her to ask if he had sent the money, Belinda told me he had wired it that day. When I asked how much he had sent, she said, "Sixty-five thousand dollars." Added to the twenty-five thousand dollars we already had received, that not only was what was needed but also left enough extra to pay that month's two-thousand-dollar water bill as well as several other unforeseen bills.

It took the money one working day to clear the bank. The man wired it on Friday, so we could not close on the hospital on Monday. But Tuesday at 12 noon, the money did become available, and I got a cashier's check for eighty-five thousand dollars. At 1 p.m., I handed the company's agent a check in front of the hospital, which we now call Solomon's Porch Retreat Center, a place of wisdom and healing.

When I gave the agent the check, his eyes got big. He said, "You sure are a man of great faith!" I replied, "This has nothing to do with me, but it has everything to do with the Father." In the months ahead, he called me from time to time to ask, "What has God done now?"

Over the next months, I had many stories to tell him about what God was doing. One was about how God provided the furniture for Solomon's Porch. We had the building, but no furniture, so we prayed. Not long after that, the manager of a luxury hotel in Gatlinburg, Tennessee, called to say his hotel was refurbishing and to offer to donate all their current furniture. Other furniture came through a friend in South Carolina who had access to used furniture from colleges in North and South Carolina at one dollar a unit. Between the two sources, we had enough to furnish all the rooms of Solomon's Porch, plus we had furniture left over to distribute to people in the community.

Soon after that, a church's senior adult group asked if they could "redo" one room. Other churches offered to "adopt" rooms, and soon the entire building was renovated and decorated. It was more than Belinda and I could ever have dreamed. In the first seven years after Solomon's Porch opened in 2002, more than 21,600 volunteers and guests stayed there.

For Belinda and me, that experience was not a leap into the dark, but rather a step into the light of the truth of 1 John 5:14-15: "Now this is the confidence that we have in Him, that if we ask anything according to His will, He hears us. And if we know that He hears us, whatever we ask, we know that we have the petitions that we have asked of Him." God wanted to provide safe, comfortable housing for the volunteers whom He would call out and send to Lynch. We were merely His conduits for that to happen.

A fourth faith principle we have experienced is that God always has our best interests at heart. Many people have asked us how we handled "giving up" so much when we left Mississippi to move to Lynch. We always reply that we did not give up anything.

Not long after we moved back, friends came to visit us. They later told us that they cried after seeing the town and the house in which we were living. But there was no need for tears. Our friends thought we had sacrificed so much to gain so little, but the reverse was true. In reality, we sacrificed so very little to gain so very much. We have learned that anything God has in mind for you and me is always far greater than anything we could ever leave behind. And anything God has in mind for you and me is always far greater than anything we could every dream or imagine.

> Anything God has in mind for you and me is always far greater than anything we could ever dream or imagine.

After all, how could driving a new luxury car or living in a five-bedroom estate home on a lake ever be better than seeing God provide in ways that only He can do? Take the story of the shingles, for example.

The second summer we were back home in Lynch some local people asked if we could put a roof on the house of an eighty-six-year-old African-American World War II veteran. At the time, the leaking roof of his house was covered with a blue tarpaulin. Every time rain fell, he had to shuffle around his little home, trying to avoid the water that poured into every nook and cranny. By that time, when people asked me for things I had learned to reply, "I don't know if I can help, but if God provides, I'll be glad to help." And so that is what I told the people about the roof.

Shortly after that, a woman from Georgia called to set up a mission trip. Just before she hung up the phone, she asked me a question. By that time, I also had learned that God can say some amazing things through a person just before he or she hangs up, so I had learned to listen carefully to the last few words of a call. Here's what the woman asked: "By the way, you wouldn't need any shingles up your way, would ya?" I immediately knew in her words was a word from God that He was providing the shingles for the veteran's roof, so I replied that I had a house right then that needed some shingles. She said she had 248 squares to give us. I told her to bring them to Lynch, and we'd put them on the man's house.

Obviously, I didn't know much about shingles. I didn't know that 248 squares is a semi-truck load until she told me—and that's enough for a whole bunch of houses. I told her to bring them anyway. I thought that God must have a use for so many shingles or He wouldn't give them to us.

There, however, was one slight problem. The woman didn't have a way to get them from Georgia to Harlan County. So I said to her, "Well, surely God wouldn't give us the shingles and not give us a truck! We'll just go to Him and see what He says." We would wait for a word from God.

His word came quickly. That Friday night, a man from Western Kentucky called to say he had heard about our ministry the night before at a meeting of area churches and that God had impressed him to call me to ask if he could pray with us about anything. I did not have to be a rocket scientist to figure out what was happening. I knew this was another word from God. I said, "Yes sir. You can pray that God will provide us a semi truck to go to Georgia to pick up some shingles a lady has given us and bring them back to Harlan County."

On Monday, he called back to say God had answered our prayer. When I asked how, he said that a young man who recently had become a Christian had been in the worship service when he had asked for prayer for a truck to transport those shingles. The young man had called his dad, who was a trucker and was on a run in California, to tell him about the need. The dad told his son that he would be glad to go to Georgia and pick up the shingles.

That man drove all the way from California to Georgia, picked up the 248 squares of shingles, and brought them to Harlan County, Kentucky, at no cost to us. As the shingles were being unloaded, I shared Jesus with him. Three months later, he became a Christian. I believe he had seen God do something that he could not explain. I know I did, and I know that beats cars and houses any day.

Oh yes, over the next months volunteers used those "extra" shingles to provide roofs for ten other homes in the community. The bonus? The next year the company sent us more than four thousand squares of shingles.

Or how could a car or a house or any material thing ever top the experience of what God did with a man from Hilton Head, South Carolina, who came to Lynch as a volunteer? He told us that God had touched his heart and called him into the gospel ministry, but that he did not know what to do next.

By that time, Belinda and I had learned that we did not need to give an answer but rather ask a question. "What is it that you do?" I asked. He replied that he was a shrimper, that he and his family had been in the business a long time, and that he had two shrimp boats. I then asked him, "What has God laid on your heart?" He replied, "Well, really I just shrimp all the time. Usually on Sundays after church I go down, check on my shrimp boats, and look out over the sea. I see all those sailboats out there. One day, God touched my heart. I thought, 'If I just had a sailboat, I could go out there and tell folks about Jesus while they are sailing around.'"

Then he asked, "You wouldn't happen to have a sailboat in Lynch, would you?" I laughed and replied, "No, I don't, but let's pray and see what God wants to do about this."

Not long after that, a friend in Knoxville, Tennessee, called and said something like this: "Now Lonnie, I know this is going to be a strange request, and I know there is no water up in Lynch, but you wouldn't happen to need a sailboat up there, would you?" I replied, "No, I don't need a sailboat, but I know a guy who does. Bring it up, and we'll make sure he gets it."

He brought that twenty-four-foot Catamaran with the thirty-foot mast to us. Let me tell you, that was quite a sight coming up our little mountain road. But, for me, the best part was making that phone call to the man in South Carolina to tell him that God had answered his request. Plus, God had given him a trailer to haul the boat on as well. There is nothing more fulfilling that seeing a person take that step of faith into the light of the reality that God has already prepared. No car or house or personal fishing boat or any other material thing, for that matter, can top that.

> There is nothing more fulfilling than seeing a person take that step of faith into the light of the reality that God has already prepared.

What is the "step" that moves us into the light of the life of faith? It is obedience.

All my adult life, I had wanted God to do something that I could not explain except by saying, "God did it!" All my life. I did not know that the key is obedience to the word God gives us. I did not know that for God to act in our lives, we must take that step of obedience into the light.

In John 14:15, Jesus said: "If you love Me, keep My commandments." I paraphrase it this way: "If you love Me, do just as I say." In verse 21, Jesus reinforces this teaching when He says that "He who has My commandments and keeps them, it is he who loves Me." It is not the person who *says* he or she loves Jesus who really

> What is the "step" that moves us into the light of the life of faith? It is obedience.

loves Him; it is the person who *does* what He says. Here's my translation: "If you love Me, do what I say. The person who loves Me, I will love, and the Father will love that person, and I will show Myself to him or her."

And how does He do that? Jesus tells how: "If anyone loves Me, he will keep My word, and My Father will love him, and We will come to him and make Our home with him'" (v. 23). *Make Our home with him.* What a thought! If we follow Jesus' orders, then the Father and the Son will reside in us. Do you know what that means? If you are a believer, the God of the Universe and the Redeemer of humankind lives in you. That's why when you really live the faith-life, people will want to know what it is all about. You will be able to tell them that it is a life that can only be explained by the words, "God did it." It is a life that is available to all who believe. After all, it has nothing to do with you or me; it has everything to do with Him.

FOUR

## "IT HAS NOTHING TO DO WITH ME, BUT EVERYTHING TO DO WITH GOD"

*One* day not long after Belinda and I had moved back to Lynch, a man stopped me on the street to ask what we were planning to do now that we were back in town. I replied that first we were going to build a city park with hookups for recreational vehicles and public showers. I told him these would be used by volunteers who would come to Lynch to help hurting people. He replied, "I've heard that before. For fifteen years, people have been saying that they are going to come to help, but nobody ever does. And probably nobody will come now."

During those early days, that seemed to be the thinking of most folks in town. In fact, a local saying was that Lynch would soon be a ghost town and that the last person out should turn out the lights.

This thinking was not only prevalent among the townspeople but also among fellow Christians whom Belinda and I met as we attended meetings in our state. I understood what they were thinking even though most weren't as open with their doubts as that man on the street.

Just a few years before I would have thought similar things: "You have no salary, no money for ministry, no organization backing you. You have no plan, no strategy, no goals. And you say you are going to 'help people' who have so many, many physical and spiritual needs? I don't believe you."

Most people were too kind to tell us what they really thought, but we sensed they were just waiting for us to fail. They, like the man on the street, didn't think anyone would come to a place such as Lynch to help. Maybe they didn't think Lynch could be helped.

But volunteers *did* begin coming to Lynch. And resources *did* begin to pour in. And we *did* begin to provide significant help to significant numbers of hurting people. Why? Because it had nothing to do with us and everything to do with God.

Belinda and I didn't lay out a plan; instead, we prayed and watched and waited for God to show us His plan, and we prepared our hearts to receive His blessings. That day when the man had stopped me, I had replied, "That's true. You've heard that before. The only difference is that this time, God's in the mix. You'll see what He can do."

Not only was God working in our hearts, but He also was working simultaneously in the hearts of potential volunteers. Soon we began to receive calls from those whom we had contacted who had indicated an interest in working in the mountains. We also heard from others who said that for years God had laid Appalachia on their hearts and now they were ready to help. Still others said they had felt God laying a particular burden on their hearts, such as the needs of children, and they now were ready to respond.

Among those who called were doctors and dentists who had heard about the need for additional health care in the mountains. When they came to hold free medical and dental

They caught the vision: they understood that their names might be forgotten by those whom they served, but the name of Jesus through whom they ministered would long be remembered.

clinics, they saw the magnitude of what God was up to and how He was touching the community. Many of them wanted to invest their lives long-term and have continued to return to hold medical and dental clinics over the years. They caught the vision; they understood that their names might be forgotten by those whom they served, but the name of Jesus through whom they ministered would long be remembered.

For all of those volunteers, making those initial contacts with us was the result of God working in their lives. It had nothing to do with us. We were merely the vessels God had placed in Lynch to be used as conduits of His blessings.

When volunteers and resources started to come and people in Lynch began thinking of Belinda and me as "the people who will help," it would have been easy for us to revert to our former performance, make-it-happen model. We could have returned to long-range planning, with its *specific, attainable,* and *measurable* measuring stick. But we knew better. We knew what was happening had nothing to do with us and everything to do with God, and we wanted to keep it that way.

As Belinda and I voiced our conviction that what was beginning to happen in Lynch was all of God and not of any person, some of the local people began to look for God to work. They began to see God in the reality of where they lived. They began to experience what only God could do in their lives.

As Belinda and I voiced our conviction that what was beginning to happen in Lynch was all of God and not of any person, some of the local people began to look for God to work. They began to see God in the reality of where they lived.

I remember one lady who told us about a time when her children needed food, but she had no money and didn't know what she was going to do. As she was walking in downtown Cumberland, a man came up to her and gave her thirty dollars he long had owed her—money she had forgotten about. With that money, she was able to put food on the table. When she told me that story, she began by saying, "Let me tell you what God did."

On another occasion, a man who had been unemployed for six months asked me to pray that he would find a job. I told him that God already had made provision to meet his need; therefore, we just needed to be made aware of that provision. Later, he and a friend were talking on the phone about deer hunting and the friend *just happened* to mention that a newly opened factory in Cumberland was taking applications. The man applied for a job and was one of the first to be hired. He came back to tell me that he had never before seen God work so quickly. What he didn't know was that the new factory itself was a result of the prayers of godly people in that 1999 prayer meeting in the park we wrote about in Chapter Two.

Not only were there changes in the lives of individual people but there were changes in the Tri-Cities communities as well. God was at work.

Not only were there changes in the lives of individual people but there were changes in the Tri-Cities communities as well. God was at work.

One day the Chief of Police in Cumberland came to me with a strange question. It went something like this: "Lonnie you wouldn't happen to have any police cars to give a man, would you?" I replied, "No, God hasn't given me any police cars, but I'll tell you what: if God gives me any, I'll know who they belong to." Belinda and I were learning that when people came to us with specific needs, we could limit God if we said, "No, we don't have that," or we could leave the door open for God to show Himself strong if we replied, "No, we don't have that, but if God gives it to us, it's yours." We were learning that often that was God's word through us to people with needs.

That day, I told the police chief that I would pray about the need for police cars, because I believed God wanted our town to be safe and because I believed He would provide the things needed for our citizens to have a quality of life that would honor Him. I also knew the chief had a greater need than police cars: he wasn't a Christian. I asked him if I could pray with him. Right there on Main Street, we joined hands, and I prayed something like this: "Lord, this man needs to know You, and he has a need in his life that no man can meet. God, if You would be honored, would You meet the need in his life so that he will know that You are God?"

Two weeks later he called me and said, "Preacher, you will never believe what God did!" It seems the city had received some unexpected money, which was just the right amount to buy five brand new police cars. When I told him that I was glad that God had provided him with those cars, he replied that he knew it had to be God Who had done it, because I wasn't involved in it, he wasn't involved in it, and no one else was involved in it. "There is no other option," he concluded.

Because of that experience with God, the police chief became a Christian and an active member of a church in town. For a long time after that, he called those new police cars "God cars" instead of squad cars. Why? Because he had seen God do something that he couldn't explain except to say, "God did it." It had everything to do with God and nothing to do with him or Belinda or me—or any other human being, for that matter.

> The police chief called those new police cars "God cars" instead of squad cars. Why? Because he had seen God do something that he couldn't explain except to say, "God did it."

On another occasion, a businessman in Cumberland talked to me about the old Novo Theatre, which he had recently purchased. The theatre had been closed since the sixties and was in bad shape, to say the least. By that time, volunteers who had come to Lynch had repaired several public buildings and homes, so word was getting around about what was happening.

That day, the businessman asked me if I could help him repair the theatre. I asked him what he planned to do with it and told him that I was not going to help people fix up things to be used for just anything. He said that he wanted to use the theatre for community revivals, prayer meetings, seminars, gospel singings, and anything that would help tell people about Jesus. I told him to count me in and that as God led, I would assist in any way I could.

He continued with the renovation, restoring the theatre to a place of beauty. One Friday afternoon he came to me with another request, which was almost as unique as being asked to provide police cars. He said he had all his money tied up in the renovation and was almost finished with the repairs but had no money left to purchase seats.

Then he asked me this startling question: "You wouldn't have any theatre seats to give me, would you?" I replied, "No, God hasn't given me any theatre seats, but if He does, I'll know who they belong to, and I'll give them to you." That day, we prayed together about his need.

The next morning when I checked my e-mail, I found a note from a friend in Mt. Vernon, Illinois. This is what it said: "Lonnie, this college up here has ordered some theatre seats, and they are the wrong kind. You wouldn't happen to need any, would you?" I quickly e-mailed my friend to tell him to hang on to those seats.

The next day, I told the theatre owner that God had given me some theatre seats and that they were his. Then a funny thing happened. He said, "Lonnie, now I hate to be picky. But I've got all my money tied up in this thing. I cannot afford to have the seats reupholstered nor can I afford to have them altered in any way. They need to have blue upholstery, and they need to fit a slanted floor." I replied, "Well, surely if God would send us a bunch of theatre seats, He would make them the right kind."

Not long after, more than 450 brand new seats valued at approximately $100,000 arrived. They were exactly the right number; they were blue; and they fit a slanted floor. Plus, the upholstery was the exact shade of blue that the theatre owner had already used to paint the theatre walls.

The theatre opened in 2003. Since then it has been used for weddings, revivals, seminars, concerts, school reunions, youth rallies, community events, and a national interdenominational prayer meeting. A state-wide meeting of men from our denomination was one of the first meetings to be held there. Over the years since, many of those men have come as volunteers to Lynch.

Folks from all across America have prayed with Belinda and me in that theatre. It is a testament to the fact that God provides what we need when meeting the need will honor Him. When something has nothing to do with us and everything to do with God, our response can only be, "God did it. All praise be to Him."

It was three years after the seats were installed before my friend in Illinois made it to Lynch. When I took him to the front of the theatre, he wept and said, "I can't believe that God could use something as insignificant as theatre seats or a person as insignificant as I to do something so mighty."

> "I can't believe that God could use something as insignificant as theatre seats or a person as insignificant as I to do something so mighty."—*a friend in Illinois*

And in a ripple effect, the owner of the theater launched another ministry called "United for Jesus." The group provides ministries similar to those we offer. That man "got it"—it has everything to do with God, and nothing to do with any human being.

On another occasion the principal of the elementary school in Cumberland asked if we could assist in building an outdoor classroom. Shortly after she made the request, a group of farmers from a church in Ohio called to say they wanted to come on a mission trip.

When the group's advance person came to make preparations, I showed him the pile of lumber that the principal had amassed for the structure and shared the need for an outdoor classroom. There was no design plan, so the farmers drew one and then came to build the classroom.

One day as I was visiting with the group, some of the men immediately began telling me that they had thought they were coming to do "missions" and that they couldn't understand what they were doing building an outdoor classroom instead. I replied, "The only thing I know is that we were asked to help the community by providing this classroom. I don't know how God will use it, but let's leave that up to Him." That seemed to satisfy them.

In the years since, God *has* used that classroom to open other doors for ministry in the school and for sharing the gospel in the community. A bonus? A few months after it was built, the classroom won the Pride Award for the best outdoor classroom in Kentucky.

On another occasion, a man from South Carolina called to ask if we needed some church pews. I told him we didn't, but we would take them because somebody else might need them. We drove to South Carolina, picked up the pews, and put them in our warehouse where they sat for two months.

One day, the mayor of Benham told me the city was trying to redo the city council chambers because the existing seating was not adequate for the increasing number of people who were attending council meetings. He wanted to know if I knew where he could get some pews. I told him God had given us pews, and he was welcome to them. He asked me to measure the pews; they were an exact fit for the council chambers.

And what about the man who had stopped me on the street when we were preparing to build West Main Park? When work began on the park in the summer of 2000, he stopped by to watch. He saw the tents and recreational vehicles that housed the approximately 130 volunteers who were working on the park. With tears in his eyes, he said, "Preacher, they did come, didn't they?"

"Preacher, they did come, didn't they?"—*a resident of Lynch*

When your life can be explained only by saying, "It has nothing to do with me, but everything to do with God," it doesn't mean that you will sit back and do *nothing* while you wait for God to do *everything*. In fact, you will work as hard as you have ever worked.

That surely was the case when we began the work on West Main Park in Lynch. The city council asked us to put in recreational vehicle hookups for our volunteers to use and then for the city to rent out later. So, my son, a friend, and I spent days and days from sunup to sundown digging with picks and shovels so the RV hookups would be ready that summer.

For Belinda and me, that pattern of long, hard hours of work would be repeated in each of the more than twenty ministries we began. Yes, you work just as hard as you have ever worked, but the difference is that you are not trying to build your own reputation or your own organization; instead, you are working in response to what God has told you to do. In the process, you are learning a different kind of planning.

For all the years before God touched our hearts, Belinda and I had done strategy planning. That's where you set a goal, write objectives to meet that goal, and then work hard to meet those objectives. Of course, you have to "tweak" the plan as you go along. You are deemed "successful" when the goal is met. In essence, strategy planning is all about you.

And then, Belinda and I experienced living by faith and learned to do responsive planning. That's where you already know what God wants to do; therefore, you know what is going to happen and respond to what God wants to do. Responsive planning is all about God—and He never has to be tweaked.

> With strategy planning, we get what we can do. With responsive planning, we get what God can do.

With strategy planning, we get what *we* can do. With responsive planning, we get what *God* can do.

To illustrate, Belinda and I don't plan a certain number of projects for the year and then hope people will show up to complete the projects. We don't plan projects and then enlist people, either. Instead, we wait until someone calls and tells us what his or her group wants to do. Then we plan for what they will do when they come, because we believe God has already been at work in their hearts. He has given them a burden for what He wants them to do in Lynch based on what He wants done in Lynch. Simultaneously, they prepare to come and we prepare for their coming. We work diligently with our ministry directors so that things will be in place for the volunteers to minister effectively when they arrive. That is responsive planning.

To plan responsively means you work in sync with God's plan to extend His kingdom. No longer do you work and work and work and then say, "Let me tell you how God let me do this." Instead you say, "Let me tell you what God did," because you know that only He could have brought the things to pass. The story about how God provided money for building supplies illustrates responsive planning well.

When we first started repairing homes and public buildings in the Tri-Cities area, we had volunteers who were burdened to help, but we had no money to buy supplies and no source for free materials. One volunteer team asked me to secure fifteen thousand dollars worth of lumber for a project they wanted to do the following month.

I had no money, and I was not known in the business community; still, I went to every lumber company in the county with the same story. I told them my wife and I were missionaries who were helping people rebuild their lives and homes in Jesus' name. I said we had no money, but we needed to open an account in order that we could buy materials for these projects. I told them that when God gave us the money, we would pay them.

You can imagine the response. In every case but one, I was laughed at. But that one store manager was all God needed to show Himself strong. That day, the man set up an account for us. The first week, we bought $7,500 worth of material; the second week, we bought another $7,500 worth. The third week, the manager called to ask when we were going to pay our account. I told him that when God gave us the money, we would know it was for the account. He said that was fine. The following month, the volunteer team arrived on schedule. To my surprise, they brought a check for fifteen thousand dollars—the exact amount needed to pay our bill. I didn't have a clue that they had planned to pay for the supplies; they had never indicated they would.

But the story didn't end there. Later that year, a church in our county asked us to help them build a building after the commonwealth of Kentucky had taken theirs for a road site. The church had enough money for materials but not for labor, which our volunteers were happy to provide. Their building was constructed for $278,000, and every cent was spent at the store that had given us that line of credit. God rewarded the faith of that store manager.

A second example concerns another park. After we had built the facilities in Main Street Park in Lynch, the Lynch City Council asked if we could assist in upgrading the park on Creekside Drive. A group from a church in Georgia had already asked to do a community project and had indicated that they had three thousand dollars to spend, so this was a perfect fit. When a member of the group came for a pre-mission visit, we surveyed the area to assess the possibilities. We told him we would like to put a children's play set in the park, so he said he would look for a set that would cost three thousand dollars.

On his way home to Georgia, the man found himself driving behind a semi truck with a logo and a phone number for a playground equipment company in another state printed on its side. He immediately picked up his cell phone and called the number. When he reached the president of the company, he told him what his church wanted to do for the children of Lynch, Kentucky, and said he had three thousand dollars to spend.

Then something happened that only God could do. The president said that he would send a catalogue, the Georgia group could pick out any set they wanted, and the company would not only donate it but also would ship it free to Lynch. The group picked a set that was valued at ten thousand dollars. They came, built the park, repaired and painted the fence around the park, installed the playground equipment, and held a Backyard Bible Club in the park for twenty children. There had been no strategic plan, only the response of God's people to what He wanted them to do, including the response of the team's advance man to what God literally placed in front of him. It had nothing to do with any of us and everything to do with God.

When you live with the sure knowledge that it is God who is acting, you look to Jesus, not any person, as your model. Before I understood this, I

When you live with the sure knowledge that it is God who is acting, you look to Jesus, not any person, as your model.

often pointed people to successful people as models. To be honest, I even pointed them to myself. In those years, I encouraged people to emulate what others were doing, and I was sure that would help them attain the results they desired. I even wrote how-to manuals that laid out step-by-step plans for attaining goals and being successful. I honestly thought that if people completed steps a, b, c, and d, they would automatically succeed. And if they failed, it was because they didn't follow the manual to a tee. It never once dawned on me that they would become more confused and discouraged if what the manual told them to do didn't work. Instead, I blamed them.

How this fit into my understanding of salvation and how to live a life that would please God went something like this: you become a Christian, and then you learn how to do "God stuff." And the way you learn to do "God stuff" is by emulating the people who are most successful in doing what you want to do.

For example, if you want to be pastor of a large church, you take as your models the pastors of large churches. If you want to be an active layperson, you take successful laypeople as your models.

If you are a pastor and you fail to meet your "success" goals, then you resign and move on. If you are a layperson and you fail, you simply say it must not have been God's will in the first place, and you move on to the next activity or program.

Of course, in those years I never looked to pastors who were not success-driven as models. I assumed they weren't accomplishing anything worth emulating.

I was reminded of how I thought during those years when a woman in Ohio e-mailed me in late 2009 to say she still had a Bible that she had used when she was a teen. In it, I had signed my name and written, "Make it happen for Jesus." I obviously

> In biblical terms, success is to let God be God; it is to know that nothing is about us, but everything is about Him.

wanted her to think *she* could make things happen and that God would be pleased when she did. I now know that such a thought process incorrectly defines success. In biblical terms, success is to let God be God; it is to know that nothing is about us, but everything is about Him.

When your life can be explained only by saying, "It had nothing to do with me. It has everything to do with God," then people will see God and not you. He will be their role model, not you. They will begin to look *for* what God is doing, not look *at* what you are doing. Living the faith-life is all about Him, not you; and if you have Him, you will find that is enough.

## FIVE

~~~

# "IF YOU HAVE HIM, THAT IS ENOUGH"

*Each* morning when Belinda and I awaken, we get out of bed, raise our hands to God, and we each pray, "Lord, all my hopes, dreams, and aspirations, all my plans, I submit to You today. Help me to see what You want to do today." Uplifted hands are a universal sign of surrender, and we want to begin each day submitted to God.

When we moved to Lynch in 1999, we were convinced that if we surrendered all we were to God, He would be all we would need. "Lord, if we have You, that is enough," we had prayed when God had said, "You won't have fancy cars; you won't have a big house; you won't have an almost six-figure salary and lots of perks. In fact, you won't even have a salary. But you will have Me and that will be all you will need."

That was fine with us. By then, we believed God would take care of us. We weren't expecting nor wanting anything for ourselves; instead, we were hungry to do what God wanted and not something we would dream up. We wanted to find Him adequate to provide all that we would need. We wanted to focus on how He would use us to bless others and draw them to Himself. Our heart's desire was—and is—to understand the ways of God so that we might walk with Him.

Since then, we have learned that to live in the reality of God at work in our lives is to live in the reality that He is indeed all we need. He is not an add-on; He is all-in-all. While this is the most basic principle of living by faith, it is also the most difficult to grasp and apply. It is not about just trusting that a need will be met, then believing hard enough and praying long enough and trusting deep enough in order to twist God's arm into doing what we have asked Him to do. In fact, it is not about focusing on the need or the provision of the need, but rather it is about focusing on the *Supplier* of the need. It is all about God. It is the surety that the provision for meeting the need is for the purpose of expanding His kingdom and bringing glory to Him and Him alone. It is about *experiencing* God as enough.

> To live in the reality of God at work in our lives is to live in the reality that He is indeed all we need.

For Belinda and me, to experience God as enough has been to trust Him to be sufficient to meet the physical needs of the people in our community. After God had led us to the great assurance that He is enough, people began to approach us with a variety of needs. We knew we didn't have the resources to meet the needs, so we took them to God. Always, we found Him to be sufficient.

When we face such basic needs as food and clothing, we know we cannot in ourselves meet those needs. We know that only God can, and He does. He is enough.

For example, not long after we returned to Lynch, we learned that about 98 percent of the children in the Lynch public school were on the free lunch program. Typical of the story of many of the children is that of one young lad who cut his lunch hamburger in half, ate one half, and wrapped up the other half and stuck it in his pocket. When his teacher asked him why he was not eating the entire hamburger, he said that his mother had told him to bring half home so that his little sister would have something to eat that night. That hamburger would be all both children would eat all day. We knew many adults, too, went to bed hungry each night.

Such stories broke our hearts, so we began asking God what He wanted to do. Our prayer went something like this: "Lord, since You fed two million people in the desert with manna, surely You can feed mountain people who are hungry and don't have any food." We didn't know how He would meet the need, but we knew that He would. And He did in ways we could never have imagined.

As we trusted the Supplier, He sent the supplies. In the early months of our time back in Lynch, we had begun distributing small amounts of donated food at the Freedom Center through our food ministry.

One day a woman came asking for bread, but we had none to give her, so Belinda took her to the store and bought her some. After Belinda returned home, she couldn't get the woman out of her mind.

*As we trusted the Supplier, He sent the supplies*

She went to our bedroom, got on her knees, and talked to God about the situation. Her prayer went something like this: "God, You said that You are the Bread of Life. These people need bread. And if they need bread, then we need bread to give them, so in Jesus' name would You provide the bread?" For Belinda, the need had become a God-given burden, a burden that only the Supplier could meet.

Twenty minutes later the phone rang. A woman in Knoxville, Tennessee, was on the line and said something like this: "You don't know me, but I have heard about your ministry. I am executive director of Bread of Life, and the Lord has instructed me to bring you a truckload of bread." The Supplier had been at work in her heart as well as in

Belinda's heart. That day, He linked the two in order to provide bread for many people in our area. That day, He began something so much greater in scope than anything we could ever have imagined, for every month since that day Bread of Life has sent a truckload of bread.

Now, Manna House, our food distribution center, distributes about $25,000 worth of donated food each month, which translates to more than $300,000 each year—and we have never had to ask anyone for food. God knows the need. He knows what He wants done. He is the Supplier; He is enough.

Also, we learned through the school system that when many children in our area go home after school, they are unsupervised and are left without any food to eat. As Belinda and a Catholic nun began to pray together about how God wanted to meet that need, He led them to begin an after-school feeding program, which later we named "Kid's Café." Again, God was enough as food came in for the program without any solicitation.

During the school year, Belinda, the nun, and other volunteers prepared hot meals for as many as fifty children five afternoons a week. They also provided Bible games and other activities for the children. Through that experience, they learned about the need for after-school tutoring and exercise, and a well-rounded program was begun for the children at Cumberland Elementary School. In the early years, Kid's Café was held in the Catholic church in Cumberland. Eventually, the feeding program moved to the Cumberland Boys and Girls Club and continues there to this day.

In 2007, we began addressing the need for food for school children to eat on weekends through a ministry called "Sacks of Love for Children." Each Thursday or Friday during the school year, elementary school children are given back packs filled with nutritious foods that they can prepare themselves. On Monday, they bring the packs back to school to be refilled later in the week. Approximately three hundred children receive this food each week. Again, we have never asked anyone for food or for money for this ministry; instead, the great "Manna Provider" provides. He is enough.

Food, however, wasn't the only obvious need. You will recall the story of our first Christmas party back in Lynch, which we recounted in Chapter Two. Our hearts broke on that cold December day as we saw children arriving barefoot, wearing shorts and short-sleeved garments. God burdened us with their need for adequate clothing. We could not meet the need, but God could—and did.

Soon, people began calling to ask about the needs of the people in our area. We always told them about the need for warm clothing. Almost immediately, loads of clothing and household items began to appear.

One of our most heart-warming experiences occurred when a woman from a church in Lexington, Kentucky, called to ask specifically about what the children in our area needed. We told her that they needed shoes. The people of that church provided five hundred pairs of new shoes and sent several women to distribute them. When Belinda went to assist them, what she saw was incredible. Those women were removing the old, tattered shoes from the children's feet. Then they were washing their feet and putting new socks and shoes on all those precious feet.

Not long after that, a high-end clothing store in another town closed its doors and gave us all the remaining stock. Some children received some expensive clothing that day.Another day, a woman in Northern Kentucky called to ask if we could use denim jeans. By then, we had learned to be specific in our response, so I told her we could use the jeans if they were in good condition, had no holes, and didn't have paint all over them, since plenty of cast-offs had come our way and we didn't want any more of those. She replied that the jeans were nice. And were they! She had connections to a jeans manufacturer in Cincinnati, Ohio, and could get brand new jeans free. Over the next three years, that company donated about $150,000 in jeans, shoes, and bib overalls, which we distributed in several communities in Eastern Kentucky.

For Belinda and me, to experience God as enough has been to trust Him with the growth of the ministry. It has been humbling to see *God* grow the ministry. After our first six months of waiting, He began opening so many doors that we

It has been humbling to see God grow the ministry.

could hardly keep up. Within nine years, more than twenty ministries had begun under the umbrella of Meridzo Center Ministries, Inc. We both worked in every aspect of each of the ministries until God sent full-time volunteers to oversee them.

Typical of how God has grown the ministry is the story of Calvary Campus.

One day, a man from Cumberland called to say he was hosting a man from Florida who wanted to see our facilities. As I showed him around, he said he wanted me to come to Cumberland the next day to meet a man from Texas who had flown in just to talk with me. I thought that was strange, since the nearest major airport is three and a half hours away; immediately I recognized that God was up to something unusual. Why else would a man from Florida and a man from Texas go to all that trouble to talk with me?

The next day I met with the two men and briefly told them about what God was doing in our area. They were very affirming of what was happening. And then they said they would like to show me something.

The following day, they took me to Blackey, which is about forty miles over Pine Mountain from Lynch. They showed me a beautiful twenty-five-acre college campus that had been built in 1916 as a preachers' school. The school no longer existed, and its eight buildings were now in a state of disrepair.

For three hours, as I listened to them talk about the history of the school, I could not figure out what they wanted. Finally, I asked them why God would want me to see all this. Did they need help in fixing up the buildings? What did they want? Why me?

Then, the answer came. The two men said they were the only remaining trustees of the school, they were getting up in years, and they didn't want the state to get the property. Instead, they wanted it to be used for ministry to the people of the mountains. They said they had heard about our ministry and that God had led them to talk with me. Then one of them said, "All you have to do is say 'yes' and all that you see is yours." I said, "Okay. I'll take it." Some things you just don't have to pray about. If God gives you a twenty-five acre college campus, you'd better be prayed up so you will know what is happening.

The next question the men asked was most unusual. They asked what I planned to do with the campus. There I was, having just been given a college campus that I had no idea I was going to get, and now they were asking for a plan on the spot. I thought for a moment and then I said, "I don't have a clue, but the same God who just gave this to me is the same God who will tell me what to do with it."

I left there in awe of how God had worked. Nothing happened for several weeks. Then, a professor at a Christian college in Dallas, Texas, called to say that someone had told him I might be able to help with something God had laid on his heart. It seems he had been in Whitesburg, about thirty miles north of Lynch, working with the area's sizeable deaf population and had sensed God's leading to start a school for the deaf. When I asked him if God had told him where the school was to be located, he replied that He had not; however, he said it would be great if the school could be located somewhere between Whitesburg and Hazard. Imagine his surprise when I told him that just a few weeks before, God has given us a college campus located midway between those two towns. Through that professor, who by the way did not come back to the area, God alerted us to the need for ministering to the deaf of our region.

Since that time, on what we named Calvary Campus, volunteers have hosted week-long day camps for as many as sixty-three deaf teens at a time, and deaf ministers have led evangelistic meetings geared to deaf teens and adults, which have resulted in many professions of faith in Jesus as Savior and Lord. Volunteers have led baseball camps and sponsored community events on the campus. Also, the Pastors' Learning Center has opened on the site to help meet the need of area pastors for more training in biblical studies. To date, thirteen pastors have taken classes at the center.

Other ministries, which we have written about in previous chapters, include the Freedom Center, Manna House, Kid's Café, Solomon's Porch, medical missions, dental missions, and home repair. Others include Club 180 for teens; The Stables at Creekside Glen Equestrian Center; Shekinah Village; Scents N Such candle making; a sewing ministry; Second Chance Surplus to provide inexpensive building supplies for area residents; the re-opening of a closed church, which is now named Community Christian Center; a furniture warehouse; training for heavy equipment operators; an adult literacy program; Backyard Bible Clubs; and a chapel on Lake Cumberland in a nearby county. True to the meaning of the Greek word *"Meridzo,"* all the ministries have provided "care" for the people of our region of Appalachia.

For Belinda and me, to experience God as enough has been to trust Him with the maintenance of the ministry. The fact is this: if a person begins a ministry, then that person is called upon to maintain that ministry, which involves caring for the facilities, providing necessary funding and physical materials, paying the utility bills, supervising programming, and providing staff salaries and benefits. Usually, when a person comes to the point that he or she feels it is no longer possible to maintain the ministry, it is shut down—and often the reason given is that God was not in it in the first place.

But when God begins a ministry, He maintains it. When He expands it, He takes care of it in ways only He can. What a relief!

> When God begins a ministry, He maintains it. When He expands it, He takes care of it in ways only He can. What a relief!

At Meridzo, God has provided money for utilities, supplies, the personal and housing needs of long-term volunteer staff members and their families, and the improvement and maintenance of the properties. He has provided more than thirty thousand short-term volunteers. And He has sent us long-term volunteer co-workers as well. To date, thirty-nine full-time long-term volunteers have stayed as long as six years. While with us, most have worked forty-to-sixty hour weeks. God has used them in mighty ways. Also, some of the long-term volunteers have gone on to work as volunteers with or to form other ministries in other parts of Eastern Kentucky. Looking back, only God could have done all that. Even in our "make-it-happen" days, Belinda and I could never have dreamed of nor devised a plan for all that has occurred in Lynch. God has proven time and time again that indeed He is always enough.

For Belinda and me, to experience God as enough is to trust Him with the future of Meridzo Center Ministries, Inc. From the beginning, our basic understanding has been that the ministries aren't ours, but God's. He originated them, and He will expand them according to His desire. Granted, He may change the form as needs change, but the original intent to help others in Jesus' name and to improve the quality of life of the people in the mountains will remain the same.

In 2007, after the number of ministries had grown to approximately twenty, Belinda and I became convicted that we were to release some of them into the capable hands of the full-time volunteers whom He had sent to oversee those ministries. While reading Matthew 16, the passage in which Jesus talks with Peter about the "keys to the kingdom," I felt God telling me that it was time to give away some "keys," as it were.

We met with our staff, told them what God had said to us, and then asked if any of them might be ready to assume responsibility for some of the Meridzo ministries. We assured them that we would always be available when they needed us. That year, we released seven ministries, confident that we could trust God to be enough to continue those ministries without our input since the ministries were His, not ours anyway. It has been exciting to see how God had continued to expand those ministries through the hard work of those dedicated volunteers. For example, Club 180 for teens has purchased a larger facility and the leaders have created several new ministries to help meet the needs of area teens.

For Belinda and me, to experience God as enough has been to trust Him when opposition has come our way. Unfortunately, when God begins to bless your ministry, some people do not understand and will even openly oppose the work God is doing. And, in our case, some have done just that. Some have been jealous of what God has done through us and have used that jealousy to try to undermine God's work. Others who do not fully understand how we can live by faith have opposed us on principle; they can't believe that we help people "for nothing," as they say. They think there must be a hidden agenda, and so they have never really trusted that God is working through us.

We have chosen not to defend ourselves publicly; rather we have chosen simply to continue with the work God directs us to do. No matter what opposition has come, He has always shown Himself to be more than sufficient to plead our case.

For Belinda and me, to experience God as enough has been to trust Him with our personal finances. Over the last decade, He has shown us many, many times that He is sufficient to meet those needs. People often ask us how we pay our personal bills since we have no salary. The answer is that whatever God has sent us from faithful pray-ers and obedient servants has always been more than sufficient to cover our living expenses.

Many, many times when we have needed money to pay a bill, a check has come in the mail with a note saying that the sender had been praying for our ministry and had felt God instructing him or her to send a check. We have never asked for donations, but God has always provided. For example, one day when I had just finished paying our monthly bills and saw that we had seventy-eight dollars left in our checking account, I turned to Belinda and said, "God sure is good to us." When she asked what I meant, I replied, "Well, this month He has given us seventy-eight dollars more than we needed." That was not a flippant remark. It was an affirmation that God had provided more than enough.

People often ask us how we are able to drive nice vehicles. The answer is that God provides them through His people whom He has blessed financially. The answer, also, is in our definition of "nice." I remember a time in our early days back home when Belinda was scheduled to attend a meeting in one part of our state and I was scheduled to speak in Illinois on the same day—and we had one vehicle. As the meeting date approached, we prayed something like this: "Lord, we don't have to go anywhere, but if You want us to go to these two meetings, make us aware of how You are going to provide for us to go."

Two weeks before the appointed day, a man called to say his truck had been on the market for a long time and hadn't sold, so he had come to the conclusion that God wanted him to give it to us. I told him I would take it. It never crossed my mind that a fifteen-year-old diesel truck full of rattles with 178,000 miles on it would *not* make the fourteen-hour round trip to Illinois and back. After all, God had provided it and what He provides is always enough. I didn't need a new luxury vehicle; I just needed four wheels and a motor. That's "nice" enough for me.

And that truck? We put another 170,000 miles on it. The truck I now drive (in late 2009) had 50,000 miles on it when it was given to us; to date, we've put another 170,000 on it, and it's still going strong. God knows our schedule and our transportation needs long before we do, and He has always provided. Our task is to use every vehicle that He gives us to bring honor and glory to Him.

Belinda and I live in the assurance that God is enough. In that assurance, we have found that God always provides; He knows the needs of the people in our area before we do. We are merely the link between the need, the provision, and the Great Supplier. Therefore, when someone asks Belinda or me for help, it is a no-brainer to reply, "I don't have it; but if God gives it to me, I'll know who it belongs to. It belongs to you."

## SIX

⁓

# "I DON'T HAVE IT; BUT IF GOD GIVES IT TO ME, I'LL KNOW WHO IT BELONGS TO"

*It's* a simple, yet profound statement: "I don't have it; but if God gives it to me, I'll know who it belongs to." Sometimes I wonder how many times Belinda and I have said that in our ten years in Lynch. When people have come to us for help and we have had nothing to give them, that response has been more than mere words; it has been a statement of faith in God, the Great Supplier. In His time and in His way, we knew that He would provide. We were to wait on Him, watch for His provision, and give Him the credit when the provision came.

Over the years, we have learned that as the Great Supplier, sometimes God sends the provision *before* we learn about the need. When that happens, He expects us to hold on to the supplies until He lets us know what He wants us to do with them. But more often, He sends the provision *after* we learn about the need. When someone asks us for something that is a legitimate need and we don't have a way to meet it, He expects us to respond, "I don't have it; but if God gives it to me, I'll know who it belongs to." The faith principle? God wants us to know that He will not ask us to give anything that He will not provide. And whether He provides *before* or *after,* God expects us to be the conduits of His grace.

Many of the stories we have shared in this book are illustrative of how God has sent the provision *after* we learned about the need. Stories such as the hedge trimmers and the seventy-five dollars (Chapter Two); Solomon's Porch and the shingles (Chapter Three); the police cars, sailboat, theatre seats, and outdoor classroom (Chapter Four); and food for Manna House (Chapter Five) are but a few examples. The stories that follow also illustrate this.

> God wants us to know that He will not ask us to give anything that He will not provide.

It has been my practice on visits to the city halls in the Tri-Cities to tell the employees to let us know if we can help them, and as God gives us the liberty to help, we will. One day when I was paying bills at Cumberland City Hall, the mayor told me the city needed white exterior paint for a city building but didn't have the money to buy it. I told her I didn't have any paint, but if God gave it to me, I would know who it belonged to.

A few days later, a friend from the University of the Cumberlands, my alma mater, in Williamsburg, Kentucky, called to say he had food for Manna House if we could pick it up. When my assistant and I arrived at the university, our friend asked if we could use some paint as well as the food. He said he had four pallets of white exterior paint we could have if we wanted it. Of course, we took it. We already knew who it belonged to; we were merely to be the delivery men. When we got back to Cumberland, we gave the mayor all she needed and had enough left over to paint some of our Meridzo buildings as well. Her response was, "The Lord sure is good."

On another day when I was at Lynch City Hall the mayor asked if we had carpet he could use in City Hall. I told him we didn't, but if God gave us some, we would know who it belonged to.

That weekend, I went to Ohio to speak. While there, an old friend whom I had not seen in years took me out for breakfast. As we were getting reacquainted, I asked him what line of work he was in, and he replied that he owned a carpet warehouse and distributorship. Sensing that God had gone before me, I immediately told him about the need at Lynch City Hall. He asked me to call the mayor and find out how much carpet was needed. I made the call and in a short time, the carpet was cut and tied to the top of my old 1986 truck. I drove seven hours back to Lynch with that carpet hanging over the cab.

God had put me in the right place with the right man at the right time with the right resource to meet a need He already knew existed.

When the mayor saw the carpet, he could hardly believe his eyes. But I knew what it was all about: God had put me in the right place with the right man at the right time with the right resource to meet a need He already knew existed. The carpet had belonged in Lynch City Hall all along.

A deacon in a local church called to ask if we could help a young woman who had come home one day to find that her drug-crazed husband had removed every piece of furniture from their house, sold it, and left town. Destitute, she and her two young sons had moved into a low-income housing unit, but she had no way even to buy a bed. I told the deacon that we didn't have any furniture, but if God gave us some, we would know who it belonged to.

A week later, a man from Western Kentucky called to say that he wanted to bring us some furniture. I didn't ask what he had but just told him to bring it all. Among the things he brought were two twin beds and a nice bedroom suite.

When the deacon, my son, and I took the furniture to the woman, we saw that she had been sleeping in a sleeping bag on a piece of plywood set on top of concrete blocks. Her sons had slept in sleeping bags on soil-stained carpet under her make-shift bed. For me, that confirmed that those beds we were delivering belonged to her. Again, God provided *after* we knew the need, and He did not ask us to give something He would not provide.

After we had set up the furniture, I asked permission to say a few words. This is what I said: "When you lie down tonight and your head hits that soft pillow, remember that God has provided you with something that even Jesus did not have. Scripture says He had no place to lay His head." She began to cry. As I talked with her about Jesus, she became a believer.

During our first Christmas season back home, an elderly widow called to say she had forgotten to pick up her medicine from the local pharmacy, and now darkness had fallen, snow was piling up, and she was afraid to drive to get her medicine. She wanted to know if we would pick it up and take it to her, which we did.

When the woman came to the door, she wanted to give us ten dollars. Belinda told her we didn't want it, that we were just glad to help her out as a way of sharing God's love with her. When the woman persisted, Belinda suggested she give it to her church's mission offering. The woman responded, "You're missionaries, aren't you?" When Belinda said, "Yes," the woman dropped the money in the snow and said, "Then take it and give it to someone." Belinda took the ten dollars.

But that was not the end of the story. Before the woman had called, Belinda and I had planned to walk around in the beautiful snow and stop to eat at the local pizza parlor; therefore, after we left the woman's house, we headed out to eat.

As we entered the pizza parlor, we saw a man whom we knew moved from apartment to apartment and was often homeless. When we asked him how he was doing, he replied that he was freezing. He said that the wick had burned out in his old kerosene heater; therefore, he didn't have any heat in his apartment.

Before we sat down to eat, Belinda and I took him to the local hardware store to buy a wick. The store had one wick left, which cost $9.95. That was a nickel less than the widow had given us. God knew the need *before* we did and used that sweet woman to provide.

———

When we were renovating our home, we needed to replace several broken windows. We had no money, so we began to pray. Not long after, someone called to tell us that a man in South Carolina had some windows to give away. I called him and he asked us to come to his place and choose the windows we needed.

We drove to South Carolina; Belinda made her choices from a stack of new name-brand energy-efficient windows, and the man arranged to deliver them to us. We went home happy, thinking that God had provided just the right windows for our home. But God had much more in mind. We thought we were getting just a few windows for one house, but the man sent a semi-truck load!

Just as with the story of the widow, there also is more to this story. When we arrived back home, we set about unloading the windows into a warehouse in Cumberland. As we were working, some people who were passing by asked what we were going to do with the windows. They asked if they could have some for their church. Of course, we agreed.

Soon, by word of mouth, people from other churches asked for windows. The result was that we were able to provide windows for five churches. God had a bigger plan than just windows for our house, and He provided the resources to carry out that plan *before* we knew the windows were needed in those five churches.

In December 2000, a man in Lexington, Kentucky, called to say he would like to bring some new toys for us to distribute at Christmas. We knew God was in this because many parents had stopped us on the street to say they had no money to buy toys for their children for Christmas and to ask if we could help. The man brought a sixteen-foot box truck filled with the toys.

We had not yet set up a structure for distributing toys at Christmas, so I played Santa for the next month. I donned a Santa cap, went to the grocery store in Cumberland, and looked for children sitting with their parents in automobiles. Then I pecked on the car window and said that I wanted to give a gift to each child in the car. You can imagine how the little faces lit up. To this day, I meet mothers who tell me that their daughters have never forgotten the dolls they received that Christmas. God knew the need before we did, and He provided.

Early on in our time back in Lynch, Belinda and I bought an old car in order to have a means of transportation for a trip we needed to make. We drove the vehicle on that trip and then for a year and a half—and had trouble with it the entire time.

During that time, a young woman came to work with us for three months. As she prepared to return to college, she asked us to pray with her about her greatest need, which was a car. As we prayed, God told us to give her our car. We obeyed, telling her about all the problems we had experienced. She gladly received the car—and drove it for three years without any difficulties. God knew the car belonged to her long before we bought it.

Our faith lesson? Don't discount what is in your hand, even if it is a clunker. You don't know what God will do with it. After all, He's a great mechanic.

> Don't discount what is in your hand, even if it is a clunker. You don't know what God will do with it. After all, He's a great mechanic.

Another faith lesson? If God gives you something and then tells you to give it away, don't be concerned about how you will replace it. Just give it away. He will take care of your needs. After we gave the car to the young woman, God provided another car for us.

A third faith lesson? Before you decide to discard something or sell something, wait to see what God has in mind. He may be preparing you to provide a resource *before* you even know the need.

Not long after we had returned to Lynch, Belinda said she wished she had a million dollars to give away in Jesus' name. After ten years back home, she now says she doesn't need a million dollars; she just needs to be a conduit through whom God can channel much more than a million dollars. We both have learned to rest in the assurance that when we know how God works, we must wait on Him to provide, because His provision is already a done deal.

SEVEN

# "IF YOU ONLY KNEW WHAT GOD KNOWS, IT WOULD BE A DONE DEAL"

*Does* God know what He wants to do in Lynch? Does God know what He wants to do in your town? Does God know what He wants to do in your life? In your family? The obvious answer is, "Yes." Then, what is the problem? It is that we do not know what God knows. If we only knew what God knows, it would be a done deal. If He knows, and we want to do what He wants done, then the question becomes this: how do we find out what He wants?

The answer is found in Matthew 7. The process of getting in touch with what God knows and what God wants to do in Lynch— or anywhere or in any believer's life, for that matter—is prayer. In the passage in Matthew's Gospel, we find the means through which believers can become aware of what God knows and wants to do in their specific circumstances as well.

In the passage, Jesus says: "Ask, and it will be given to you. Seek, and you will find. Knock, and it will be opened to you" (Matt. 7:7). To ask, to seek, and to knock are *not* three ways of saying the same thing, as many people think. Rather, to ask, to seek, and to knock is a three-stage process of finding out what God knows and what He wants to do in our lives. If you must always ask what you are to do next, it is because you don't know what God knows. Once you know what God knows, the answer to that question will be settled.

*Ask*. What should we ask? How should we ask? How can we know if what we want to ask is the will of God? These are questions believers often ask. Belinda and I have found that following the Matthew 7 process of prayer helps us with these questions; it helps us weed out selfish prayers and focus in on prayers that please God.

> To ask, to seek, and to knock are *not* three ways of saying the same thing, as many people think. Rather, to ask, to seek, and to knock is a three-stage process of finding out what God knows and what He wants to do in our lives.

When Belinda and I are faced with a need and want to know what God knows about it, as we pray about the need, we ask ourselves three questions: is this prayer unselfish in nature; does this prayer honor God; and, is this prayer biblically correct?

*Ask:* When Belinda and I are faced with a need and want to know what God knows about it, as we pray about the need we ask ourselves three questions: is this prayer unselfish in nature; does this prayer honor God; and, is this prayer biblically correct?

First, we ask: is this prayer unselfish in nature? Scripture teaches that God does not answer selfish prayers unless those prayers line up with His will. We all know we are self-focused by nature, so this question is extremely important. If you don't believe you are self-focused, consider this simple illustration: when you look at a group photo that includes you, who do you look for first? Yourself! Given our innate self-centeredness, before we can pray with the expectation that God will answer, our hearts must be cleansed of sin and self, our motives purified, and our will tuned to His.

Second, we ask: does this prayer honor God? Is its intent to honor Him or just to make us feel good? In other words, who does it highlight? Who will receive the credit for the answer—God or us? God does not share His glory with anyone. . . neither you nor me.

Third, we ask: is this prayer biblically correct? Is it consistent with prayers in the Bible and with biblical teachings on prayer? God does not answer prayers that are not in harmony with what He teaches through His Word. A word *from* God is always consistent with *the* Word *of* God. The *will* of God will never contradict the *Word* of God. Often, when we ask this third question, we are compelled to dig into Scripture and to listen for the Holy Spirit's guidance as we study; we hunger to know what God knows as revealed in His Word.

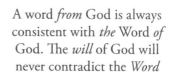

A word *from* God is always consistent with *the* Word *of* God. The *will* of God will never contradict the *Word* of God.

For Belinda and me, the *asking* stage in the process of prayer works like this: it would be very easy for us to be overwhelmed by the needs we see every day in Lynch, since there will always be needs we cannot meet and people whom we cannot help. Left to our own devices, we could not know what needs to tackle. But we aren't left to figure that out. God already knows what He wants us to do; therefore, we just need to know what He knows.

After we have used the three-question litmus test, we wait to see if God will translate that need into a specific burden that we can't shed. If that happens, then what we are to do is settled. What a relief that is! We don't have to wonder what to do next. Our responsibility, then, becomes obeying God as He shows us how He has already planned to meet the need. The stories we have shared in this book are but a few of the many that illustrate this stage of the prayer process.

⟿

*Seek.* To seek is to look intently for something specific. It is to be alert to the possibility of finding it. It is to watch with purpose. When you seek/wait on God, you watch Him connect the dots of what He has already told you that He will do. The problem for many believers, however, is that they don't have a clue what they are seeking from God.

> *Seek:* When you seek/wait on God, you watch Him connect the dots of what He has already told you He will do.

To help believers understand this, I often ask this question: "If God could do one thing in your life that you would know to be of Him and Him alone, what would that be?" One thing. One specific thing. When James writes in James 4:3 about asking "amiss," he is talking about praying for everything generally and nothing specifically. Think about this: if you don't know what you're looking for from God, you could already have it and not know it! Or think about this: if you don't know what you're looking for from God, He could give it to you and you wouldn't even recognize it!

Remember the parable of the lost coin? The woman who lost it looked for one specific coin. And the parable of the lost sheep? The shepherd searched for one specific sheep (Luke 15). Just as the woman expected to find the lost coin and the shepherd expected to find the lost sheep, so we must live each day expecting God to do specific things in and through our lives that only He can do.

Belinda and I try to live each day expecting God to show up and when we can't see Him our prayer is, "Lord, cleanse our hearts and make us ready to see You. Lord, we just want to see You show up. How you manifest Yourself is up to You, but Lord, we surely do want to see

Your manifestation in some way and in some form where we are today. Lord, let us see You today. We want to know what You know; we want to see what You see."

This principle became etched into my life in 1992 a short time after Belinda and I had talked with Henry Blackaby. A church in our association of churches in Ohio had closed its doors, sold the building for twenty-five thousand dollars, and given the money to our association to be used to start new churches. One day the director of the association called to ask if I would chair the committee that would oversee the expenditure of the funds. I agreed and promptly forgot all about it.

A few weeks later a local pastor called to ask if our church would assist in raising five thousand dollars to purchase a mobile home in which to begin a Bible study in a nearby mobile home park. The goal was for the Bible study eventually to become a church. I agreed.

In the past, every time I had asked the people of the church for money for similar projects, it had been a done deal. So I went before the people and said something like this: "We have a great opportunity to be involved in mission expansion. Brother John called and said he needs five thousand dollars for the project, so today just speak to the Lord and let Him speak to you. Then drop whatever He tells you into the offering plate at the back door. We'll raise that five thousand dollars, and we'll have a new church in our community soon." I went about my way, confident that the money would be given.

Later that week I asked the church financial secretary how much we had received. "Zero," she replied. "Wait. You mean nobody gave a penny, not even me?" She said, "Nope. Nobody gave anything." I was stunned. Instead of going out for lunch that day, I went to my office and got down on my knees and prayed something like this: "Lord, I don't know what is going on. I've never had this happen before, and You are going to have to teach me what is happening." His response came clearly: "Lonnie, you need to quit praying about the five thousand dollars, because three weeks ago, before the need even came to you, I gave you charge over twenty-five thousand dollars."

I had not been watching for God. I had been in my own little world. My heart was out of sync with God's heart. I had asked "amiss." When God had answered, I didn't even know it. That day, I promised God this: "God, if I ever ask You for anything, the next thing I'll do is watch to see how You do it. If I'm going to ask You, then I am going to assume that it's going to get done. If I doubt that it's going to be done, then I'm not even going to ask. I am not going to waste Your time or mine trying to ask You for something that I am not going to watch to see it show up. I am going to watch until You do it, or I die." That became my prayer from that day forward.

Seeking not only involves watching, but it also involves waiting. When God brings a need to our attention, it may take some time for Him to rearrange our lives in order that we can see what He already has prepared. It isn't that He needs to rearrange any *thing*; rather, it is that He has to rearrange us, the people whom He will use to meet the need, and those who have the need.

For some women in our mountain community, seeing the fruits of that process took years. One of the women gave testimony to that in a church service after Belinda and I had shared why we felt God had brought us back home. With tears streaming down her face, she stood to tell how she had walked the streets of Cumberland for eleven years, praying that God would send someone to help. Her testimony opened the floodgates as another woman then stood to say she had been praying for seven years and another for five years.

Indeed, the seeking/waiting step in the process of prayer can seem interminable. For Belinda and me, the average time between when God burdens us with a need and the time He meets that need has been

> For Belinda and me, the average time between when God burdens us with a need and the time He meets that need has been two and a half to three years.

two and a half to three years. Remember Solomon's Porch? That took three years from the time the need became a burden until the time God unfolded His plan.

We waited even longer to see God unfold His plan for an equestrian ministry. I love horses and have had a horse most of my life, so when we moved from Mississippi, I brought my horse, Crystal, with me. Back home in Lynch, I loved to ride Crystal along the road. When I did, parents would ask if their children could pat her. I began to be impressed that something to do with horses would be a great ministry, and so I began to ask parents if their children would like to ride. Of course they wanted to, and so up and down the road we went, with me leading Crystal as the children rode. A good relationship-building ministry, I thought. But I didn't know what God knew. He had something much bigger in mind, something that would take several years to unfold. We were not to have a one-horse ministry.

People began calling to offer us horses, seemingly out of the blue. Soon, we had not one, but four, which I housed in a nearby barn.

Then one day a man told me he thought I needed some land for the horses. So I asked him to join me in praying to see what God wanted to do. I told him I was content with the current situation, since the owner of the barn where I was boarding the horses wasn't charging me. I told him that I would wait to see what God knew that we didn't.

It didn't take long. A week later the man came back to tell me he had bought us a farm. I was amazed that he had returned so quickly and even more amazed that he had known the land was available. He had bought twenty acres. To be honest, I couldn't imagine what twenty acres would look like in the mountains. As I have said, Lynch is one hundred yards wide and two and a half miles long with the 4,145-foot peak of Big Black Mountain and Pine Mountain converging on its eastern end. I couldn't help but think that the horses would either have to have two short legs and two long legs or they would have to run around the side of the mountain.

Obviously, I didn't know what God knew. He knew that an equestrian ministry didn't have to be located in Lynch, and that fifteen miles north of Lynch were twenty flat acres perfectly suited for His plan. (Eventually, we would obtain an additional thirty-five acres adjacent to the twenty acres.) God knew that, in time, volunteers from a church in Kentucky would build a barn valued at eighty thousand dollars. He knew that by 2009, we would have been given eighteen horses, a donkey, and a llama. He knew that in 2009 alone, more than 150 teenagers would participate in day camps at The Stables at Creekside Glen Equestrian Center that we built on the site and that autistic children from a local school would come regularly to participate in activities at the center as well.

God also knew we would need someone to manage the growing equestrian ministry, which after all was His idea in the first place. For nine years we prayed for that person—and for nine years I, my son, and other volunteers mucked stalls, hauled hay, and trucked water. Then in His time, in 2009 God sent a seminary-trained full-time volunteer and his wife to oversee the center. Now, the center offers day camps, trail rides, and a ministry to autistic children. The director also teaches equestrian management courses at a local college and plans to begin a cowboy church.

It also took nine years for us to know some of what God planned to do with the fifty-five acres. In the summer of 2010, we plan to open a youth camp called Shekinah Village on the property. Another full-time volunteer couple oversees this ministry. The village includes five cabins around two lakes, a western store, a recreational vehicle park with six slips, and the outdoor Gethsemane Theatre. Church groups have constructed and decorated the cabins. They have built the western store, the RV park, and the theatre. Now we wait to see what God already has planned to do with Shekinah Village, "a dwelling place of God."

In all of this, what God knew He would do was so much bigger than we could ever have imagined. In all of this, God revealed His "done deal" in His time as we waited on Him. Had we not waited, had we moved on our own schedule, we would have missed the plan of God. We would never have known what He knew. In all of this, however, God did not show us all He knew at one time; instead, He unveiled His plan one piece at a time. God isn't into instant gratification. That, too, is a principle of the faith-life.

To say that seeking involves waiting sounds contradictory, but in God's plan, it is far from contradictory. To wait on God is not to be inactive. It's not sitting around twiddling your thumbs and worrying about what to do next. It's about perseverance; it's about being ever-mindful of God; it's about getting in tune with what God knows. It's about doing what He places in front of you. And, perhaps most importantly, it is about strength-building for the next stage of the process of prayer: knocking. The prophet Isaiah says it best: "They that wait upon the Lord shall renew their strength" (Isaiah 40:31).

*Knock.* Knocking implies action. When you seek/wait on God, you watch Him connect the dots of what He has already told you that He will do. After you see that God has connected all the dots, then you know exactly what to do next; it's time to act. The faith principle is this: don't do anything until you see God do something; then, when He does something, you will know exactly what you are to do. That is knocking.

*Knock:* After you see that God has connected all the dots, then you know exactly what to do next; it's time to act.

This faith principle is best illustrated through how Club 180, the teen center in Cumberland, came into being.

One Saturday night, Belinda and I were sitting in our truck in the parking lot of the Family Dollar Store on Main Street in Cumberland, eating ice cream and watching teens cruising. As we watched, we saw cars slow down and teens pass something to the occupants of other cars. We knew we were probably watching drug deals going down. The need was obvious: our teenagers needed something to do besides cruising and drugs. That night God began the process of translating that need into a burden. He began to show us the need for a teen center. We knew that we didn't know how to start a teen center, but that God did and if He wanted it, it was already a done deal.

At first nothing happened, and so we prayed to make sure a teen center was a word from God and not merely something we wanted. We applied the three-question litmus test: is this prayer unselfish in nature; will it honor God; and, is it biblically correct?

To each question, God gave a resounding, "Yes." As we prayed, we recalled the verse in Luke 12:48: "For everyone to whom much is given, from him much will be required." We knew that every time God brings a burden of this magnitude into a person's life, He requires an equally great commitment, and we wanted to be sure we were willing to make that commitment.

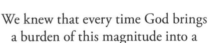

> We knew that every time God brings a burden of this magnitude into a person's life, He requires an equally great commitment.

When the commitment issue was settled, we began to watch for what God would do. For two years, we watched and waited. Finally, a man representing a church in Spartanburg, South Carolina, called to ask if any vision God had placed in our hearts had not yet been fulfilled. In his question, I heard a word from God. I immediately told him about the need for a teen center. Another principle: you have to be watching for God to act; if you don't watch, you will have forgotten all about what you asked Him before He is ready to answer. I had learned that lesson back in 1992 in Ohio when I had told God, "I am going to watch until You do it, or I die."

That day on the phone with the man from South Carolina, I described a place where our teens could come and feel safe in a non-threatening environment, where they could hang out and have a good time, and where Christian adults could hang out with them and talk with them about Jesus.

Then the man asked me to describe what I saw inside the center. I remember thinking that I really didn't know what teens like, but I went ahead to describe a big screen TV, Xbox, Playstation 2, Cube, foosball, ping pong tables, pool tables, and tables at which the teens could sit and talk and drink sodas and eat popcorn.

The man said he would pray about the things I had requested. Two weeks later, he called to tell me that he and some folks from his church were coming the following week to bring us the things I had requested. Astonished, I asked, "Bring what stuff? What kind of stuff are you bringing?" He said something like this, "We're bringing your big screen TV, your Xboxes, Playstation 2s, your foosball table. Your stuff has all been donated, and it is all brand new."

Now we had a new issue to bring to God. We didn't have a place to put that "stuff." We didn't have a building for a teen center. Therefore, I asked the man not to bring the things.

What to do? Rent a building or wait on God to show what He had in mind? We waited on God. I told the man that when God gave us a building, we would call him back. He said he would hang on to the things and would join us in praying about the need for a building.

A few weeks later, a pharmacist in town called me. He said he had just sold his business to a national chain and that as a part of the agreement, he could not operate a pharmacy in town for five years. He also said he had a three-year lease on two buildings in downtown Cumberland and wanted to know if we would be interested in using the buildings for ministry. I knew immediately this was God's timing and God's plan.

I called the man in Spartanburg and he and some of the members of the church brought all that wonderful "stuff." Club 180 Teen Center opened in 2004. The first night, 250 kids showed up. Needless to say, that first night was chaotic; but in spite of that, many of the teens made professions of faith in Jesus as their Savior and Lord.

But God wasn't finished with Club 180. Several months later, a friend in Louisville, Kentucky, called to say he had access to restaurant equipment valued at $100,000 that a Kentucky owner of a restaurant in Ohio wanted to donate to a ministry. It was exactly what Club 180 needed. Volunteers from Northern Kentucky moved the equipment from Ohio to Cumberland. With that, the ministry was off and running. Within five years, the volunteer directors of Club 180 were able to buy a permanent building that was much larger than the original quarters, which allowed them to expand the ministry.

When did Club 180 begin? The opening date was in 2004, but it really began at an unknown time in the heart of God. It was a done deal long before that opening night. Belinda and I, the church in Spartanburg, our friend in Louisville, the volunteer leaders of Club 180, and even the owner of the Ohio restaurant and the volunteers in Northern Kentucky were just privileged to get in on God's plans. Through that experience, we learned another faith principle: when a need becomes a burden, in His time God will do something only He can do—if we let Him.

*Ask. Seek. Knock.* This is the process of prayer. This is how we learn what God knows, that what He knows is already a done deal, and that we must walk into that done deal. The interesting thing is this: once you are into the flow, the process keeps repeating itself. You receive an impression, which becomes a burden. You test that burden to see if it is of God. You wait and watch in anticipation of what God is going to reveal.

Often, when you are beyond the asking stage and are in the seeking/waiting stage, God begins to show you how He is working. Often, He then will place another need on your heart, and the process begins again. Therefore, with some needs, you

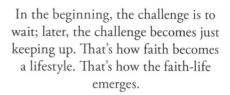

In the beginning, the challenge is to wait; later, the challenge becomes just keeping up. That's how faith becomes a lifestyle. That's how the faith-life emerges.

are in the asking stage; with others, you are in the seeking stage; and with still others, you are in the knocking stage. When you first begin this process, it may seem painfully slow, but soon the challenge becomes keeping up with all God is doing. In the beginning, the challenge is to wait; later, the challenge becomes just keeping up. That's how faith becomes a lifestyle. That's how the faith-life emerges.

I now understand what the Apostle Paul meant when he said: "You need to pray without ceasing" (I Thess. 5:17). He meant that at any given moment you can be in any of the three stages of the process of prayer and of finding out what God knows. This has been the way God has worked in every one of the more than twenty ministries that have come into being during the ten years Belinda and I have been back in Lynch.

After we had been in Lynch about nine years, I asked Belinda if we had prayed any prayers in that time that God had not answered. She thought for a while and replied, "I can't remember a time that God has not answered our prayers or has not been in the process of answering." And when He has been in the process of answering, we have waited until He did. After all, if it is settled with Him, it is a done deal.

# EPILOGUE

$A$ volunteer who came to help us in Lynch told me our approach to our food ministry was all wrong. He said we were giving away too much food. Citing an old adage, he said that we should be teaching people to fish, not just giving fish to them.

This is what I told him: "As I recall, that is a Chinese proverb, not a biblical story. So let me go to my Father and see what He has to say."

I prayed intently, listened for God, and this is the Word I heard from Him: sometimes it is necessary to give a person a fish, because that's the only way he or she will survive; and, sometimes it is time to teach a person to fish, but only when he or she is ready to learn. But what good does it do to teach a person to fish and then put him or her in the desert where there is no water? My conclusion was that we not only are to give people food and teach them to fish, but we also are to help them build lakes in which they can fish.

As we have trusted God to provide for the immediate physical and spiritual needs of the people with whom we have been privileged to work, so we have trusted Him to provide "lakes" for their long-term needs and to produce a quality of life that will honor Him. As God provides, those "lakes" in which our people can "fish" are being built.

"The poor and needy are thirsty, but there is no water.

But I, the God of heaven, have heard them.

I will make a river to flow from the mountains

so that all men will know that God has done this thing."

Isaiah 41:17, 20 (Lonnie's paraphrase)

All praise be to God. Amen.

# RESOURCES

To order the following resources, visit
**www.meridzo.org**

*Miracle in the Mountains:*
*Experiencing the Transforming Power of Faith in the Heart of*
*Appalachia (Book)*
by Lonnie and Belinda Riley with Joyce Sweeney Martin

*By Faith: Living in the Certainty of God's Reality (Book)*
by John Franklin and Lonnie Riley

*Miracle in the Mountains (CD)*

*Faith: The Journey to Spiritual Transformation (a set of five CDs)*
Messages by Lonnie Riley

⌒

To order the following resource, contact
LifeWay Church Resources Customer Service, Nashville, Tennessee
Phone: 800.458.2772
E-mail: orderentry@lifeway.com
Website: www.lifeway.com

*Experiencing God Kit,* by Henry and Richard Blackaby and
Claude King;
includes six CDS with testimonies, including that of Lonnie Riley

⌒

For further information or to get involved in Meridzo Ministries,
contact
**Meridzo Center Ministries**
P.O. Box 425
Lynch, KY 40855
Phone: 606.848.2766 (office)
606.733.0329 (cell)
E-mail: Lriley98@bellsouth.net

# About the Authors

**Lonnie and Belinda Riley** are the founders of Meridzo Center Ministries, Inc., in the heart of the Appalachian Mountains in Eastern Kentucky. They live in Lynch, Kentucky. Previously, Lonnie served as the assistant director of evangelism for the State Convention of Baptists in Ohio; assistant to the president of the University of the Cumberlands in Williamsburg, Kentucky; and pastor of churches in Ohio, Kentucky, and Mississippi.

Lonnie received an associate of arts in civil engineering degree from the University of Kentucky, Southeast Campus; a bachelor of arts degree from the University of the Cumberlands in Williamsburg, Kentucky; and did further study at The Southern Baptist Theological Seminary in Louisville, Kentucky. He is the co-author with John Franklin of *By Faith: Living in the Certainty of God's Reality*.

Lonnie and Belinda have three adult children, Lisa, Brian, and Amy; and a son-in-law, Jeremy. They also are the proud grandparents of six grandchildren: Allisa, Gabrielle, Jesika, Gavin, Macie, and Gracen.

**Joyce Sweeney Martin** is an author, editor, and writing coach in Louisville, Kentucky, where she and her husband, Larry, live. She is the author or co-author of five books, including *Faith Works: Ministry Models for a Hurting World* and *Team Jesus: Planting Churches the Master's Way*.